Destiny

Also by Rowena Pattee Kryder

Emerald River of Compassion
Sacred Ground to Sacred Space
Faces of the Moon Mother
Moving with Change
Gaia Matrix Oracle

DESTINY
Gaia Matrix Oracle Numerology

Rowena Pattee Kryder

Golden Point

Mount Shasta, California

Library of Congress Catalog Number: 95-075697
ISBN 0-9624716-8-2

Book design, illustrations, and cover illustration by Rowena Pattee Kryder
Printed in the United States of America

*This book is dedicated to the hundreds of people
this New Earth numerology has spoken to.*

Acknowledgements

I want to thank my dear friend Alma Rose for her interest and support and Linda Webb for her editing.

Contents

We are all in a Trust, a divine trust to Earth.
Destiny can only be found by love and wisdom.
Imprisoned by our senses, and our beliefs,
we put those who frighten us behind bars.

Interior liberty is what is needed to find destiny.
The non-conformity of our souls is unique to each of us.
To be possessed of cosmic consciousness is to be free.

DESTINY

Destiny is possible; fate is probable.

The numerology in this book is a pattern of possibilities; not a prediction nor a prophecy. *Gaia Matrix Oracle* numerology is predicated on the awareness that your name and birthdate are vibrational information coded by numbers and linked with archetypal meaning.

First, I will establish a distinction between how I use the term destiny as opposed to fate. Destiny is the potential fulfillment of the order of who you are. Fate is the hapless falling away from that order—moving toward entropy (the tendency toward chaos) and the laws of time. Destiny implies you have the gnosis of self inherently and consciously. Fate, on the contrary, is the result of ignorance.

The Greek word for fate was *moira*, which Anaxagorus said are "particles" or "allotments," infinite in number, and which are the constituents of the primal elemental qualities of *aether* and *aer*. The moira are the disposition of sub-atomic nature to attract and repel, combine and separate—to evolve through a determinism that is always within and all around us insofar as we are a part of nature. The moira are also connected to *sperma*, "seeds," the tendency of a particular potency to unfold.

1

According to Greek myth, the moira decree everything. They decree that mortals shall die and that human bodies be made in a certain way in resonance with their souls. Incarnation is determined, fixed fate. Even the hour of death is fixed by the moira. Only Zeus, the sky god, is privy to what they determine—for aether and aer make up the sky, and hence Zeus can read the signs of the "seeds," the tendency of things to come. This does not mean he could *alter* or choose the things to come.

Do we have the capacity, within the powers of fate, to have some degree of free will? Or must we fulfill the "seeds" of fate that the Hindus call karma (the concept that what we send out comes back, and that we eat of the field of our own 'previous' actions)? It is my viewpoint, as expressed in this book, that fate has a firm hold on us insofar as we don't know ourselves and refuse to face karma, refusing responsibility for our lives. But insofar as we reflect on and reveal who we are, we can balance our karma and come into our destiny. Numerology is one method of knowing who we are. Fate—the moira—will then become part of the momentum of our destiny, like ocean waves; but we can choose the *direction* of our course—like a captain steering a ship in the ocean.

Numbers have the vibratory potencies of the moira as "particles" and "allotments." As we shall see, there are numbers that reveal purpose, others that reveal synchronicities and yet others that show cycles of recurrence. (I call these numbers teleos, synchronic and cyclic respectively).

In Greek myth the moira were eventually reduced to three entities who had specific functions dealing with the threads of fate. Clotho was the spinner, Lachesis, the measurer and weaver, and Atropos, the cutter of the threads. Clotho corresponds to the subliminal and largely unconscious forces of nature within us that we *feel*. Lachesis corresponds to the perceptions we have of an apparently "objective" world. Atropos corresponds to perceptual mortality in cognition as well as the death of our feeling. The "spinning" aspects take place in time that we experience as biological cycles and rhythms (heartbeat, breath, digestion and excretion, waking and sleeping). The "measurement and weaving" aspects take place in perceptual space, the realm of our senses (seeing, hearing, smelling, tasting, touching—the basis of empirical science). The "cutting" aspects take place in the realm of ideas, the intangible cognition that transcends, "cuts off" the other two realms (mathematics, quantum physics, Platonic ideas).

As long as one or another of these three functions is dominant, we are subject to fate, but the possibility exists to reveal the unconditional and immutable quality that runs through all three, and thus become a *Light Unto Ourselves* insofar as the unconditional and immutable shines through us. This state nourishes what I call destiny, for in it we are living from a place of unconditional commitment to being who we are.

When the three functions are out of balance, fate or necessity has hold over us. When in balance, we live our destiny. To bring balance we need to become aware of the vibrational patterns of numbers in our name and birthdate—for these hold the imprints of our incarnation, based on past incarnations and karmas. By knowing ourselves, we can become free. Freedom from fate ultimately means a cessation of investment of any kind in a specific identity (as a self-image). Paradoxically, it is by knowing ourselves that we can become free of the conditions constraining us. Our destiny depends on self insight in relation to all the other factors and influences that come into our lives, including parents, siblings, school and environment. When these conditions are unconscious, they rule us. Such is the meaning of ignorance and the power of fate, the moira.

Probability holds fate in its grasp, but destiny can elude probability—for destiny implies the creative discovery of the order that lies within your true self, pure *being*. The vibrational quality of your name and birthdate are a direct link to that self and therefore to your destiny.

Self doubt increases the probability of fate or random events taking over. To erase self-doubt is to inquire and explore the *possibilities* of your destiny, not only the probabilities. Probabilities relate to human beings in general, any *en masse* events, or large numbers of peoples. There is no possibility of finding the creative course of your destiny in a method of probabilities.

For example, it is highly improbable that you or I even exist. Your I is intentional. The unconditional and immutable quality running through creation has found a way to resist the entropic disorder so that the intentional message of your destiny reaches its destination more or less as it was sent. Interpretation may vary, but the message of being a human being is loud and clear. A human being is capable of letting the eternal Light shine through. The uniqueness of being you is less clear if you have no way to attune to your inner essence, your true self and possible destiny. Your destiny is born through time, but is seeded in eternity, where the unconditional and immutable qualities lie. Numerology is one way to attune to your inner essence seeded in eternity.

The fulfillment of your destiny is dependent upon your recognition of an archetypal as well as an absolute reality which is the source of spacetime and which also permeates it. The relation of the physical to the spiritual is interpenetrating. The body is spiritual and can be understood vibrationally as one with your destiny. Consciousness knows more than it is taught. Trusting intrinsic knowing is the key to education and the unfoldment of your destiny. Your destiny comes from eternity, but in time it is up to each of us to create and reveal it.

Part One
METHODS

Gaia Matrix Oracle (GMO) numerology involves your whole birth name and birthdate as well as any spiritual name you might have. In GMO numerology, there are two major ways of determining the correct readings for your full birth name: 1) Chronological and 2) Harmonic.

Chronological Method

In the chronological method you discern more about the *timing* of the unfoldment of your destiny. Your first name delivers the vibratory qualities of the first part of your life that corresponds to *involution* in a cosmic perspective. Involution represents the qualities coiled up like a spring in your karmic disposition or incarnational potential. It springs forth at birth and unfolds in childhood. It is through the unfoldment of your intrinsic potential that you can recognize involution within yourself. It is best known through intuition and feeling.

The middle part of your life may start in puberty, your first Saturn return (29 years) or later. How can you know when the middle part of your life begins? In the Path Readings, the path between the numbers corresponding to the first two letters of your second name will give you a clue as to *when* the middle part of your life began (or will begin). This middle part of your life corresponds with *evolution* in a cosmic perspective. In the middle part you release your potential in maturing ways that enable you to develop individuality and increased perception.

The greater (enlightenment) potential of your later years can be recognized by the path corresponding to the numerical vibration of the first two letters of your *last name*. This name was most likely passed on by your parents. The implication is not that all of your ancestors have the same destiny, but that they have the same *potential* to bring forth their wholeness

5

and greatness. In history, those who learn from their ancestors gain insights and weed out redundancies from what they inherit. This is the *sacrifice* phase of the cosmic cycles.

The last cosmic phase, called *eschaton*, is used only for those names that truly represent a spiritual initiation in your life. A complete balance of the fates (moira) is implied through the powerful vibrations of a spiritual name.

In the chronological method, you use the following table to obtain the correct numbers up to nine:

ENGLISH LETTERS REDUCED TO NINE NUMBERS

1	2	3	4	5	6	7	8	9
A	B	C	D	E	F	G	H	I
J	K	L	M	N	O	P	Q	R
S	T	U	V	W	X	Y	Z	

Step One:

Write the number above each letter of your name. For example:

```
1 1 4  5 1    8 9 7 8 3 1 5 4    4 6 3 7 3 1 1
J A M E S    H I G H L A N D    D O U G L A S
```

Step Two:

Whenever two identical numbers occur immediately adjacent to each other, as in this case 1-1, it means you have an archetype that is a guardian or ally for as long as you use that name. Look up the corresponding number (In this case, the number 1 in general, and 1 Creator in particular) under Path Readings. To get a more extensive reading on the archetypes, see the GMO *Gaia Matrix Oracle*.

6

In your *first name* the relevant archetypes are:

1 Creator   2 Primal Waters   3 Kingdom   4 Priest/Seer
5 Immortals 6 Antagonists   7 Primal Pair 8 Trickster
9 Heavenly Powers

In your *second name*, the relevant archetypes are:

10 Shaman   11 Death Dance   12 Life Mother
13 Judge/Oracle   14 Alchemist   15 Hero/Demon
16∂ Virgin/Child   16Ω Celestial Earth   17 Synarchy
18 Golden Marriage

(Note that the two-digit numbers 10 through 18 which are paired with archetypes from the Gaia Matrix Oracle correspond to the single-digit numbers 1 through 9. Simply add the two digits of the archetype number to obtain the single-digit number that represents a letter of your second name.)

In the last *name* the relevant archetypes are:

19 White Buffalo   20 Heart of the Sun   21 Blue Pharaoh
22 Kundalini   23 Music of Spheres   24 Grail Mother
25 Black Buffalo   26 Eagle Crooked Path 27 Burning Buddha

(As noted above, you add the two digits corresponding to each archetype to obtain the single-digit number corresponding to each letter of your name.)

In any *spiritual name* you might have the relevant archetypes are:

28 Arhat   29 Gem City   30 Silver Net   31 Mother of the World

You may or may not have archetypal allies in your name. If you have one or more it simply implies you need a *constant* quality through the changes of your life as you discover and actualize your destiny. In the example given above, James has 1 Creator as an ally in the early part of his life and 19 White Buffalo at the end of his life.

Step Three:

In the case of James, *after* 1-1 (Creator as ally) he has the path 1-4.

1 1 4   5 1

J A M E S

He would look up 1><4 under the Involution Paths (See **Path Readings**) and read the meaning. For example:

1> < 4 Eternal Sacrifice

"The eternal source of creation gives everything through divine sacrifice each moment so that you can see the sacred in everything."

After reflecting on how this sentence relates to his early life, he looks up 4-5 (**4><5 Communion**) and finally 5-1 (**5><1 Spiritual Creativity**).

This procedure is used for all three phases of your name: *Involution* (first name), *evolution* (middle name) and *sacrifice* (last name). The meanings of the paths in involution arise in the early part of your life but continue all through your life. The meanings of the paths in evolution arise in the middle part of your life and continue through the later part of your life.

Note that in the **Path Readings**, 5><1 is the same as 1><5. In other words, the *order* of the two numbers is irrelevant here.

Harmonic Method

In the harmonic method you do not reduce the letters to the simple numbers through 9, but use the full-blown numbers of the letters as follows:

ENGLISH LETTERS LINKED TO NON-REDUCED NUMBERS

1	2	3	4	5	6	7	8	9
A	B	C	D	E	F	G	H	I

10	11	12	13	14	15	16	17	18
J	K	L	M	N	O	P	Q	R

19	20	21	22	23	24	25	26
S	T	U	V	W	X	Y	Z

In this method you receive more vibrational information of the numbers themselves and discern more about the in-depth quality of your intrinsic destiny, irrespective of temporal dimensions.

Look up the numbers corresponding to each letter under **Harmonic Number Readings**. In the Harmonic method each number is a harmonic of the fundamental tone of One, unity. In relation to the keynotes themselves, I use the key of C as 1 because 256 cycles per second (middle C) is the 8th octave of 1 cycle per second (c.p.s.):

c.p.s.	1	2	4	8	16	32	64	128	256 (middle C)
	C	C'	C''	C'''	C''''	C'''''	and so forth		
octave	1	2	3	4	5	6	7	8	

When I use a + sign following a keynote, it indicates the tone is slightly sharp. When I use a - sign following a keynote, it indicates the tone

9

is slightly flat. Although sounds at these frequencies are below the audible range, I use these numbers, corresponding to lower octaves, to easily relate to our numerology.

The harmonics of number (as cycles per second) correlate with musical tones as follows:

1	2	3	4	5	6	7	8	9
C	C'	G'	C''	E''	G''	Bb''	C'''	D'''

10	11	12	13	14	15	16	17	18
E'''	F+'''	G'''	A'''	Bb'''	B'''	C''''	C#''''	D''''

19	20	21	22	23	24	25	26	27
Eb''''	E''''	F-''''	F+''''	F#''''	G''''	Ab''''	A''''	A#''''

28	29	30	31	32 etc.
Bb''''	B-''''	B''''	Cb''''	C''''' etc.

By using these corresponding keynotes you can play your name on the piano or any other musical instrument. You might code the keys of the piano as follows:

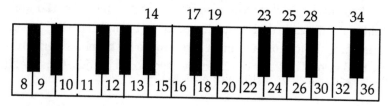

Not only do the seven octaves of the piano have numbers, but they harmonically relate to qualities of the numbers themselves—some suggestions of which are given in the **Harmonic Number Readings**.

10

Step One:

In the Harmoic method you write the actual number (not the reduced number) of each letter in each of your names, and read the interpretation under the corresponding number.

For example:

10	1	13	5	19		8	9	7	8	12	1	14	4		4	15	21	7	12	1	19
J	A	M	E	S		H	I	G	H	L	A	N	D		D	O	U	G	L	A	S

Step Two:

Read in sequence: the numbers 10, 1, 13, 5, 19, 8, 9, 7, 8 etc. under **Harmonic Number Readings**.

SOUL AND PERSONALITY NUMBERS

Step One: Separate Vowels and Consonants

To find the soul and personality numbers in both methods (chronological and harmonic) you separate the vowels from the consonants. The vowels represent your inner aspect (soul) and the consonants represent your outer aspects (personality).

Step Two: Reduce Numbers and Add

In this method you reduce any two -digit numbers by addition. For example:

$$10 = 1+0 = 1$$
$$13 = 1+3 = 4$$
$$19 = 1+9=10 = 1+0= 1$$

Add the numbers for soul and personality separately.

| 10 | 13 | 19 = (1+0+1+3+1+9) = 15 = 6 (personality) |

J   A   M   E   S

| 1 | 5 | = 1+5 = 6 (soul) |

Step Three: Read

Look up number 6 under the **Harmonic Number Readings**. In the case given above, the soul and personality are resonant (identical numbers).

Step Four: Interpret

Taking the name James as the involutionary potential, Highland as the maturing self, and Douglas as the higher (enlightened) potential, we can interpret the fact that the number 6 of the personality in the higher potential is resonant with both the soul and personality of the involutionary potential (6s); and that the soul of the maturing self (Highland = 1) is resonant with the soul of the higher (enlightened) potential (Douglas = 1). Reflect on the meaning of the number 6 as related to soul and personality.

Sometimes all the numbers are different, which implies that the unique qualities of the relevant numbers can manifest in your destiny differently through personality and soul.

OVERSOUL AND OVERPERSONALITY NUMBERS

To get the **Oversoul** number, simply add the soul numbers from the *vowels* of all the names and look up the number under the **Harmonic Number Readings**. If the number is less than number 31, use the non-reduced number. Otherwise reduce it.

1 + 5 = 6   9 + 1 = 10   15+21 + 1 = 27

J A M E S   H I G H L A N D   D O U G L A S

In this example: 6 + 10 + 9 = 25 = Oversoul number
Look up number 25 in the **Harmonic Number Readings.**

To arrive at the **Over Personality** number use the same procedure, using the *consonants:*

10 + 13 + 19 = 42 = (4+2) = 6
J A M E S

8 + 7+ 8+12 + 14+4 = 53 = (5+3) = 8
H I G H L A N D

4 + 7+12 + 19 = 42 =(4+2) = 6
D O U G L A S

6 + 8 + 6 = 20 = Over Personality number.
Look up number 20 in the **Harmonic Number Readings.**

LIFE PHASE NUMBERS

To get an overview of involutionary potential, maturing self and enlightened potential, add the soul and personality numbers of the first, middle and last names respectively:

JAMES   = 6 (personality) + 6 (soul)   = 12
HIGHLAND   = 8 (personality) + 10 (soul) = 18
DOUGLAS   = 6 (personality) + 9 (soul) = 15

Look up these numbers in the **Harmonic Number Readings.**

DESTINY NUMBERS

Finally we can arrive at the destiny number of your name by adding all the reduced life phase numbers of each name.

In the case of JHD: 12 = 3, 18 = 9, and 15 = 6.

Add 3 + 9 + 6 = 18 = **Birthname Destiny** number. Look this number up in the **Harmonic Number Readings**.

The overall number of the birthname is one indicator of your destiny. The other indicator is your *birthdate*.

In a birthdate the first level to consider is the numerological significance of the day, month and year you were born. The *day* you were born refers to your relationship to the Earth herself. The *month* refers to the lunar cycle, the qualities of which can be known more fully from the *Faces of the Moon Mother* (Golden Point Productions, 1992). In general, the months correspond to the phases of the moon as follows:

January: Sickle Moon and first quarter of Crescent Moon

February: Last three quarters of Crescent Moon and first half of Emerging Moon

March: Last half of Emerging Moon and First Quarter Moon

April: Swelling Moon and first quarter of Gibbous Moon

May: Last three quarters of Gibbous Moon and first half of Culminating Moon

June: Last half of Culminating Moon and Full Moon

July: First Waning Moon and first quarter of Disseminating Moon

August: Last three quarters of Disseminating Moon and first half of Transporting Moon

September: Last half of Transporting Moon and Last Quarter Moon

14

October: Yielding Moon and first quarter of Balsamic Moon

November: Last three quarters of Balsamic Moon and first half of
Immanent Moon

December: Last half of Immanent Moon and Dark Moon

The *year* relates to the sun, the qualities of your destiny with others
in a given year.

If James was born on January 10, 1944 then he reduces and then adds
the numbers as follows:

month		1
day		10
year	+	<u>1944</u>

$$1955 = 1 + 9 + 5 + 5 = 20 = \textbf{Birthdate Destiny number}$$

Use the largest number up to 31. In the case of James, his two destiny
numbers are:

birthdate = 20
birthname = 18

The destiny number of your *birthdate* relates to the *temporal* significance of how you relate to your time. The destiny number of your *birthname*
relates to the inner and outer quality of your whole self.

The list of numbers with corresponding archetypes follows:

1. Creator	2. Primal Waters	3. Kingdom	4. Priest/Seer
5. Immortals	6. Antagonists	7. Primal Pair	8. Trickster
9. Heavenly Powers	10. Shaman	11. Death-Dance	12. Life-Mother
13. Judge/Oracle	14. Alchemist	15. Hero/Demon	16∂. Virgin/Child
16Ω. Celestial Earth	17. Synarchy	18. Golden Marriage	19. White Buffalo
20. Heart of the Sun	21. Blue Pharaoh	22. Kundalini	23. Music of Spheres
24. Grail Mother	25. Black Buffalo	26. Eagle Path	27. Burning Buddha
28. Arhat	29. Gem City	30. Silver Net	31. Mother of World

Types of Numbers

How can you find where the various aspects of yourself fall in a total cosmogonic scheme? How do the significant numbers (destiny, soul, personality etc.) relate to each other? You can find out by noting the *types* of numbers your name or birthdate consists of: teleological, synchronic and cyclic. Earlier I referred to these three types of numbers as relating to the Greek moira called Clotho, the spinner (cyclic), Lachesis, the measurer and weaver (synchronic), and Atropos, the cutter (teleos).

When discussing the three moira, we start with the cyclic numbers and run in reverse—for time is reversible for them. Indeed they create the irreversibility of time.

In our experience, first comes the spinning and weaving of Clotho as the deep cyclic recurrences in the natural world and in our bodies that we know as feeling (the cyclic numbers of 3, 6 and 9).

Second comes the measurement of our *perceptual* self (the empirical self), governed by Lachesis through the synchronic numbers (2, 5, 8) that we know through an awareness of a coming together of similar elements (the world as metaphor).

Third we come to Atropos, the cutter who cuts off the feeling and perception, bringing about a death of limited identification and the possibility of an expanded awareness of our destiny. Through Atropos we come to a clear cognition of the meaning of our lives (teleos numbers of 1, 4, and 7). Beyond and yet through these numbers we can reveal the immutable Light that shines through us.

Teleological means purposeful direction and if you have mainly ones, fours, and sevens in your name or birthdate it implies that your incarnational destiny is to reveal meaning and truly discover your purpose in this lifetime.

Synchronic means "together time" or synchronicity, an awareness of simultaneous or similar events that have meaning. If you have mainly twos, fives and eights in your name or birthdate you are involved in sychronicities.

Cyclic means to move in cycles. If you have mainly threes, sixes or nines in your name or birthdate it implies your incarnation will unfold through repetition of similar events and a process of recurrence, and you can gain momentum through cycles.

We can see the patterns of the trinity of types of numbers by graphing them in the following way, which also reflects their relationship to a fourfold pattern of 1) source, 2) agent, 3) process, and 4) effect:

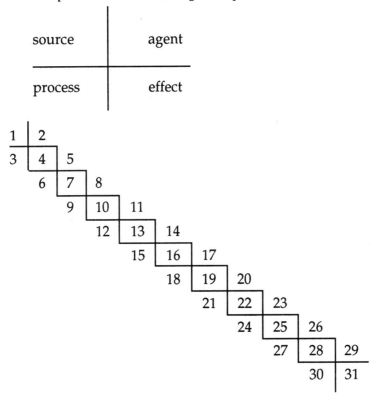

In each quadrant, the effect (as teleos number) becomes a source (except number 31, the last effect). The synchronic numbers are above (as agents) and the cyclic numbers are below (as processes).

In the GMO we see these three types of numbers also have a significance that we can reflect on in the pattern of the matrix:

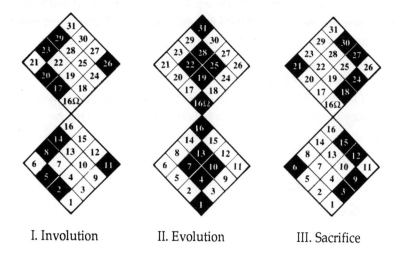

I. Involution   II. Evolution   III. Sacrifice

In order to use these types of numbers in numerology, we need to understand more deeply their archetypal and geometric significance within three phases (Involution, Evolution and Sacrifice) of nine numbers (archetypes 1 through 27) plus the additional phase of four numbers (archetypes 28-31). Here I will give an overview.

Involution

In involution, the series begins with 1 Creator and ends with 9 Heavenly Powers. If you have more numbers in this phase, it implies a deep absorption and capacity to behold the invisible and perhaps metaphysical aspects of the universe.

Teleos numbers: 1, 4, 7

The 1 Creator and the 4 Priest-Seer commune and create in order to behold the blueprint for the human body (7 Primal Pair). The purpose is the manifestation of creation and bodies from a spiritual source.

Synchronic numbers: 2, 5, 8

The 2 Primal Waters is a mystery to all except the spirit (5 Immortals) when the mind (8 Trickster) is able to be still and reflect the mystery in the mirror of the pure spirit. Often the mind cannot fathom the mystery because it is out of touch with spirit.

Cyclic numbers: 3, 6, 9

The orientation (3 Kingdom) of the plan on earth is clear when the soul (6 Antagonists) is pure in love, but when frustration and anger prevail, the lessons must be repeated in vast cosmic cycles of seasons, years and aeons (9 Heavenly Powers).

Evolution

In evolution, the series begins with 10 Shaman and ends with 18 Golden Marriage. If you have a predominance of numbers in this phase, it implies you are well-grounded and active in the world in some form of self-expression.

Teleos Numbers: 10, 13, 16∂ and 16Ω

The imaginal capacity to go into trance and bring forth sacred art (10 Shaman) has the deep purpose to awaken conscience through awareness of cosmic law (13 Judge/Oracle) and thereby to purify yourself and give birth to the divine child (16∂ Virgin/Child). The direction of this phase is to birth the New Earth (16Ω Celestial Earth).

Synchronic Numbers: 11, 14, 17

When involved in matter, with a physical body (11 Death-Dance) your destiny is bound up with all evolutionary sentience; wherein you can discover how to transmute matter in your own being (14 Alchemist) and find others who do the same (17 Synarchy).

Cyclic Numbers: 12, 15, 18

The emergence of consciousness out of the cycles of life (12 Life Mother) through seasons, years and aeons flows into the societal process (15 Hero/Demon) whereby you undergo Herculean tasks in order to bring a boon of justice to society. Through the repetition of these lessons, you bring about a fusion of opposites within yourself (18 Golden Marriage).

Sacrifice

In Sacrifice, the series begins with 19 White Buffalo and ends with 27 Burning Buddha. If you have a predominance of numbers in this phase, it implies you potentially can fully actualize the highest aspects of your being in this incarnation.

Teleos Numbers: 19, 22, 25

Taking initiative means passing through obstacles by living truth (19 White Buffalo) which activates powerful energy compelling you to surrender to the divine (22 Kundalini). This enables you to have empathetic awareness of all sentience, expanding the field of sensitivity of your finite body to a cosmic body (25 Black Buffalo).

Synchronic Numbers: 20, 23, 26

The circulation of light is both an information and energy exchange through solar ecology (20 Heart of the Sun) which simultaneously invokes the vibratory sound harmonies of the universe (23 Music of the Spheres). This gives you the capacity to acknowledge, forgive and resurrect your own soul, opening the way for others' soul resurrection (26 Eagle Crooked Path).

Cyclic Numbers: 21, 24, 27

Through the transformation of your body to a light body (21 Blue Pharaoh) your heart and mind become one (24 Grail Mother). The cycles of time are thereby understood as a shifting toward dissolution into the timeless when all lessons are learned and all karma is consumed (27 Burning Buddha).

Eschaton

Teleos Numbers: 28, 31

Through the joining of wisdom (28 Arhat) and compassion (31 Mother of the World) you can actualize not only your purpose, but the purpose of humanity and the universe as a whole.

Synchronous Number: 29

When you let beauty be your guide, you will create harmony everywhere you go (29 Gem City).

Cyclic Number: 30

There is no limitation to how everything that goes out comes around because the cosmic structure is one interwoven network (30 Silver Net) that your higher intelligence knows.

When interpreting by using the three types of numbers, the key numbers to look for are:

Oversoul number
Over-personality number
First name number (vowels + consonants)
Middle name number (vowels + consonants)
Last name number (vowels + consonants)
Name destiny number
Birth day number
Birth destiny number

In the case of any numbers you reduced (for example 30 + 51 = 81 = 9) you can look not only at 9, but at 18 and 27 (all 9s).

KEY NUMBER MEANINGS

In general the meaning of the numbers can be epitomized as follows:

1 Focus, create and initiate.
2 Move with change and the mystery of primal substance.
3 Find the cosmic axis of your life and orient yourself.
4 See, have faith and hold purpose.
5 Stay with spirit amidst the changes of life.
6 Watch the cycles of your soul's desires and frustrations.
7 Have trust in the plan and purpose of the human body.
8 Allow memory and imagination to work together.
9 Be with right timing in heavenly cycles.
10 Initiate through the imaginal and the soul of nature.
11 Enter into the density of matter and manifest what you need.
12 Be with the cycles of life and awaken consciousness.
13 Find conscience and natural cosmic law amidst trials and legalities.
14 transform, transmute and integrate.
15 Enter the cycles of societal change.
16∂ Purify and birth the light within you.
16Ω Discover paradise as a higher vibrational earth here and now.
17 Join with others who are whole and individualized.
18 Allow the cycles of the fusion of opposites within.
19 Pass through all obstacles by living truth as true purpose.
20 Circulate light as information and energy.
21 Regenerate through the development of your light body.
22 Surrender to the divine will and integrate new energies.
23 Listen to the vibrational harmonies of the universe.
24 Attune heart and mind in resonant cycles.
25 Empathize with others and expand your sense of identity.
26 Resurrect your soul through forgiveness and love.
27 Dissolve all illusions and burn through all karma.
28 Center, watch and guide with wisdom.
29 Harmonize dissonance and behold the beauty in everyone.
30 Open cosmic intelligence to the invisible network.
31 Have compassion and transmute poisons to medicines.

Part Two
READINGS

Harmonic Number Readings

Numbers represent vibratory *qualities* through a quantitative differentiation of the One. The numerical alliance with archetypes is inherent in the qualitative nature of number. The river of life flows according to the vibrations that may be experienced as sound or music. Eternity projects the plan of creation which externalizes through time as space. Number as vibrational qualities in a transcendental consciousness are emitted through the galactic center, stars and planets to Earth and into our bodies and consciousness. Our destiny is to return to the One by finding a balance of qualities within a whole—the totality equals the One.

In the following discussion of numbers, the first section of each number (listed under the *word* for the number one, two, three etc.) I discuss a number's *general* qualities. Under the following numerals 1, 2, 3 etc, I discuss the *specific* aspects of a given number. Each number is within us all, but a specific incarnation reveals, by numbers—in name and birthdate— the resonance and work to be done in that incarnation.

The keynotes are derived from 1 = C. Numerological ones are not therefore, all octaves of C, but are diverse harmonics—based on their vibrations. The geometric forms are based on centers, circles and intersections. The inherent nature of numbers and their interrelations (through addition, multiplication, subtraction and division) and their square roots— is part of the vibrational language of numerology. The geometric forms may help you receive insights on the numbers applicable to your name or birthdate.

Triangular numbers form triangles by increasing by 1 row the number below a given triangle.

For example:

3:     10:   15:

In a similar way, square numbers make a square such as

9:     16:   25:

Each is a sum of successive odd numbers. For examples 1 + 3 + 5 + 7 = 16.

ONE

●

The number one is the center, the point, the "seed" within all things—the source in involution. It is also the circle, the circumference, embracing all things in evolution. It becomes overlapping circles producing the *vesica pisces* giving birth to all things in sacrifice like a mother.

And it is the simultaneity of point and circle, of seed in fruit that at once embraces all things and dies to be reborn through every center in eschaton. Every number divided by itself remains one and one multiplied by itself remains one. Metaphysically, no number can be taken from its unity.

The one as monad is a simple spiritual principle from which all others are derived. In India it may be called Atman, the supreme spirit or imperishable Self. Others call it God (Christian), Wakan Tanka (Lakota), the Tao (Chinese), Allah (Islam). One is the fountain of all sources and only in the indivisible unity is it an absolute source.

The four archetypes that resonate to the number one are 1 Creator, 10 Shaman, 19 White Buffalo and 28 Arhat. With one, the Creator said "Let there be light." Each photon is a symbol of the one that is both a unit and unity. The 10 Shaman brings the one into vibratory sound; whereas 19 White Buffalo suggests the one movement of living truth that passes through all obstacles. The 28 Arhat is the one of wisdom that rests in repose, embracing the light of the Creator, sound of the Shaman and the movement of White Buffalo within his equanimous perspective.

25

1

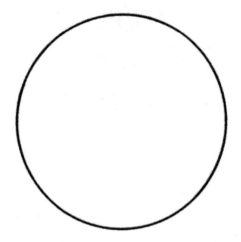

keynote of C

In truth, the human soul, along with everything else, is seeded in the Creator's heart. When the number 1 appears in your name or birthdate, you have the power to tap into the creative fountain of the source through the center of your being. This is the coincidence of the center of your humanity with the heart of creation. You can initiate projects from a true creative source. This number is exemplified in the Sanskrit *bindu* (point) which is an intentionally focused energy.

10

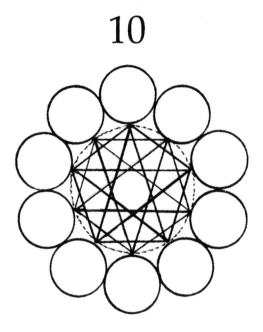

keynote of E'''

The one in the evolutionary cycle is 10, symbolizing the archetype of the Shaman. The circle is the Shaman's drum and wheel of life, containing all the vibrational harmonics of the world. The Shaman initiates the cycle of evolution in mid life. The only one of the existence axes in the GMO, this archetype suggests being able to take initiative and engender creative powers in the midst of life.

If you have a 10 in your name or birthdate you have the capacity to stay in touch with the 1 of the Creator through an imaginal reality, while also being in the stream of ordinary existence. You also have the capacity to bring your dreams into actuality—especially through sacred art.

10 is the number of the Pythagorean Tetractys and of the Kabbalistic 10 Sephiroth (spiritual principles or fountains). It is a triangular number.

The Tetractys:

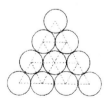

19

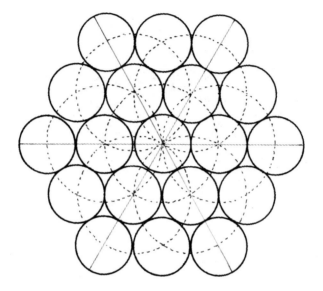

keynote of Eb′′′′

The number 19 refers to White Buffalo initiating the cycle of sacrifice. White Buffalo transforms the Old Earth cultural world into a way of *living truth*. This archetype stimulates a way of consistently asking, "What is the meaning or truth of this?" Sacrifice means "making sacred" by sloughing off all irrelevancies and falsehoods. Through resonance with the Shaman and Creator of the Old Earth, White Buffalo maintains contact with creative spirit and the soul of nature. If you have a 19 in your name or birthdate you can move through obstacles by wholly living your truth. Stay in the center of any polarities and you will find this way.

19 is a body-centered hexagonal number, and is the number of years in a Metonic cycle—the cycle of the revolutions of the moon—after which she returns to have her changes on the same day of the solar year.

28

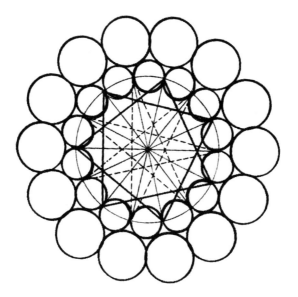

keynote of Bb″″′

The number 28 relates to the Arhat as the first archetype on the path of eschaton. In the *Gaia Matrix Oracle* this implies a transcendence of the first seven worlds. The path of eschaton is walked only by those with true spiritual names—given by a spiritual master or in some cases, received directly from within. Of extremely high vibration, those with spiritual names may contemplate, with compassion and transcendence, the seven prior worlds simultaneously (Old Earth: spiritual, human, natural, cultural and New Earth: cultural, natural, human). In a birthdate, 28 implies your capacity for wise guidance, a great perspective and caring.

Like the number 10, 28 is a triangular number. It is the same as 7! (1+2+3+4+5+6+7). 28 relates to the number of moon stations or asterisms that are constellations used as an earlier cyclic measure of time.

TWO

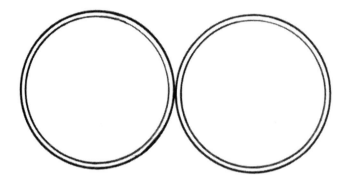

The twos express a polarity and the nature of substance and matter. The first even number, two is the *means* between one and other numbers. Whether two is seen as a straight line or two circles within a larger circle, it represents the means between One and the birth of all other numbers. It, along with all subsequent *even* numbers, is considered feminine; whereas odd numbers are considered masculine.

Two is the "Mother" number. Out of two comes the wave, and out of the wave comes the sea of vibrations. Archetypally two represents the sea of subtle energy as the primal substance (2 Primal Waters), as well as matter (11 Death-Dance), and the circulation of these vibrations wedded to light (20 Heart of the Sun). Finally the two as subtle energy is vibrationally refined in pure harmonics of 29 Gem City.

2

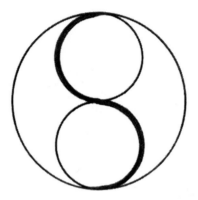

keynote of C'

The Primal Waters, an archetype of involution, expresses the primary spiritual substance of all worlds to be. The first synchronic number, 2 reveals the simultaneity of spirit and substance as subtle energy. The number 2 implies being aware of the sacred amidst mundane daily life and realizing the subtle energy in every substance. If you have twos in your birthdate or name you can be sensitive to subtle energy and enjoy the uncertainties of life as a mystery.

2, whether added to itself or multiplied by itself, produces the same number; whereas 1 added to itself produces more than by multiplication. All other numbers when multiplied by themselves produce more than by addition. 2 is also the first oblong number.

11

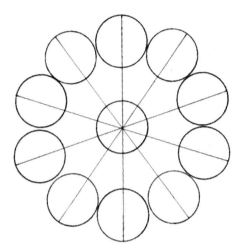

keynote of F'''

The number 11 corresponds to the Death-Dance archetype symbolizing the inherent motion of all matter or mass in the universe. This
archetype represents the density and inertia of matter itself. In daily life,
the number 11 resonates to money, exchange, abundance or loss, a sense of
wealth or poverty. If you have this number you have the power to manifest
a form, to transform or even work with destructive forces. The second step
in the phase of evolution, the Death-Dance as 11 is the most *manifest* aspect
of any of the numbers. With 11 in your name or birthdate, you need to keep
dying to redundancy and you can manifest your greatest potential.

11 makes a gnomen with five spheres radiating from one.

20

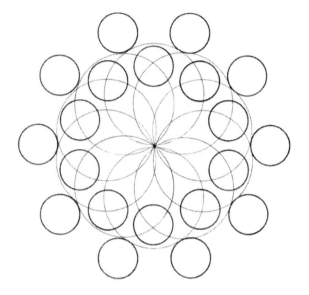

keynote of E''''

The Heart of the Sun archetype vibrates with the number 20 and is the second step in the phase of Sacrifice. Here matter is revealed as pure light, and the circulation of light and subtle energy throughout the natural world. This implies light is revealed as the true exchange system or "money" of nature, and if you have a 20 in your name or birthdate you are empowered to circulate this "money". Solar ecology is this archetype's subtitle, which implies a right and balanced distribution of light in the environment as well as within. You are a spiritual and nutritional messenger. In daily life, the number 20 implies working with light, color or information as exchange mediums of the planet as a whole.

29

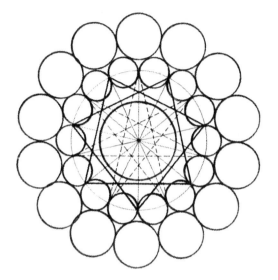

keynote of Bb+''''

The second step in the phase of eschaton is the number 29, referring the the archetype of Gem City. Here light is revealed to be crystallized harmonic patterns that reverberate throughout all worlds. An agent in the New Earth Spiritual World (8th world), Gem City provides the means for spiritual substance to be realized as pure lattices of light and harmonics of sound. If you have 29 as a spiritual name it implies that you are a way-shower of harmony. In a birthdate, 29 implies that you have the potential to draw forth the harmonies of the universe through working with color, sound, movement and form.

29 is the approximate period of the moon's revolution (29 days, 6 hours, 40 minutes).

THREE

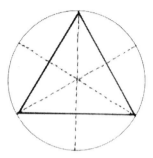

The threes bring forth processes of vibration that reveal relationships between opposites. Three is a cyclic number that brings orientation amidst change. The cosmic axis becomes established as an energy center around which life circulates. Orientation is possible with a triangle through the differentiation of base and height. Three also represents the means, middle or relationship between two.

The trinity is at the heart of innumerable traditions as the primary level in which one and two manifest themselves: Christian: Father, Son and Holy Spirit; Hindu: Brahman, Vishnu and Shiva; Chinese: *I Ching* Trigrams made of broken yin and unbroken yang lines. In alchemy there are three fundamental principles of Sulphur, Mercury and Salt; and in physics it is found that the sub-atomic particles called "quarks" have fractional charges of plus or minus 1/3 and 2/3.

In the 3 Kingdom archetype the king, priests and warriors are differentiated to guard, serve and receive inspiration from the center that reaches to heaven as a pillar. In evolution three relates to the cycles of organic life and the feminine energies of love that weave the patterns together (12 Life Mother). In the phase of sacrifice, the cellular memory becomes intensely felt. The 21 Blue Pharaoh is the archetype of this development of the light body. This archetype initiates the release of karma through a cosmic heightening by the soul's journey through the cycles of the planets, which ends with the eschaton number 30 of the Silver Net—the cosmic intelligence and awareness of the akashic records.

3

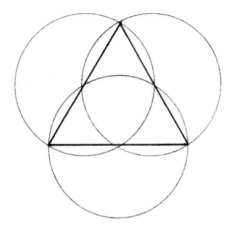

keynote of G'

The first cyclic number, three reveals the change of orientation and structure that brings forth growth and transformation (3 Kingdom archetype). This archetype implies an orientation within the structure of hierarchy. This archetype helps you to find your place in a larger whole and acknowledge priorities. The triangular pyramid is a relevant form in organization. Threes imply using the polarity in substance to find orientation to a new situation. If you have a 3 in your birthdate or name you are particularly adept in relationships and can mediate opposition.

Three is the first triangular number as well as the first gnomen.

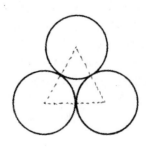

12

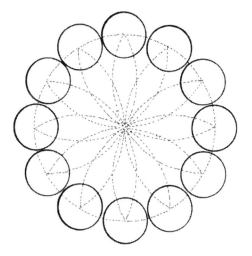

keynote of G'''

The number 12 brings forth qualities of the Life Mother—nourishment, growth, right balance and exchange with the mineral, plant and animal kingdoms of the Earth. If you have the number 12 in your birthdate or name you can involve yourself successfully in the organic life processes of the Earth. 12 implies a human consciousness working mindfully with the kingdoms of nature and also nurturing yourself.

Associated with the zodiac, the number 12 represents wholeness through a crossing of the four elements (fire, air, water and earth) with the three principles (cardinal, fixed and mutable). The 12 months of the year are representative of the 12 Life Mother archetype. 12 tribes, 12 apostles of Christ, 12 chairs in Arthur's round table and other associations imply the depth of wholeness that this number represents.

12 is an oblong number and also a circular number of 3 x 4.

21

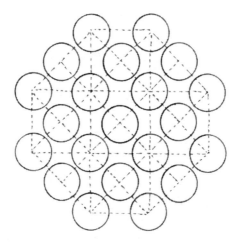

keynote of E+''''

The Blue Pharaoh archetype brings in the three of the phase of sacrifice, which implies a New Earth experience of cellular change in your body. Through the number 21 you can bring forth the subtle energy in nature and your body at once. Here is an orientation of releasing the unnecessary in your life and allowing light to live and vibrate in your cells. If you have this number in your birthdate or name you can be particularly aware of light and subtle energy whirling through your chakras. Your own alchemy depends on your capacity to transmute negativity and the density of your physical body into light through three levels of transmutation: solid, fluid and radiant.

21 is a triangular number of 6!(1+2+3+4+5+6). When an exclamation point is used after a number, it means you add numbers in a series starting from 1 up to that number.

30

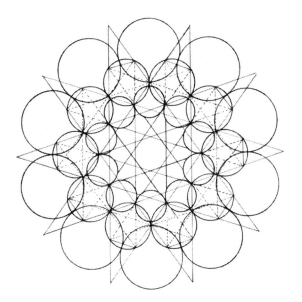

keynote of B''''

The number 30 is in the phase of eschaton (the 8th world of the New Earth: spiritual) as the Silver Net. Through this archetype you can access the Light of Cosmic Intelligence at will. Your orientation is spiritually cosmic and you can receive information at a distance that enables wisdom to be born within you. On a mundane level, this implies acting wisely in daily life. In your birthdate, 30 implies the potential to be a matrix worker, receiving patterns that enlighten the planet through appropriate orientation with others and with every situation you meet.

30 is an oblong number of 5 x 6 or the relations of 3 X 10.

FOUR

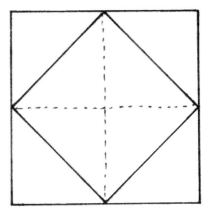

Four is a teleological number of purpose completing the intention of the number one and mediating the fulfillment of the number seven. Equally with number one, four resides on the essence axis in the *Gaia Matrix Oracle*. It is the number of discernment and fine-tuning of values, which opens the energy for fulfilling your destiny.

Four is a foundational number and is symbolized by the base of the pyramid. Alchemically, four relates to the four elements (fire, air, water, earth), four energy states (radiant, gaseous, fluid, solid), and four atmospheric conditions (hot, cold, dry, humid) that also correlate to the four humors and types of people.

Here the paradoxical phase of four functions (source, agent, process and effect) is effected as exemplified by regeneration provided by the seed (source) in the fruit (effect).

In involution four is represented by the spiritual mediator of the 4 Priest-Seer. In evolution, four functions inwardly through conscience (13 Judge/Oracle). Sin and guilt (born with judgement) are released in the phase of sacrifice wherein the four (as 22 Kundalini) is the mercurial messenger of subtle energy liberating the soul. The final four is in eschaton and brings the compassionate embrace of all spheres (31 Mother of the World).

4

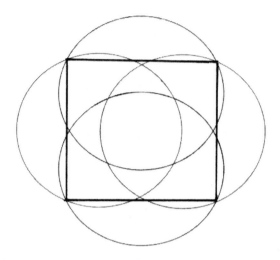

keynote of C''

As a simple 4 in involution, four in your name or birthdate implies mediating as a Priest or Priestess, the intent of the Creator through your destiny. From this vibration you can know the sacred in daily life and reflect back to your community the essence of things. You can be stable in your purpose and perceive wholeness in nature, other people and organizations. You can be a foundation stone to your group and bring forth regenerative projects and resources.

4 is the first square number. A good symbolic project is in finding how to square the circle of the one. Also you may consider the 4 as a cross.

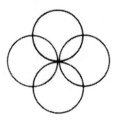

13

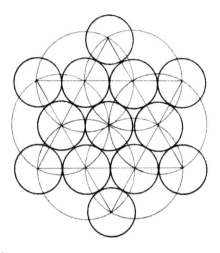

keynote of A′′′

As 13, the number four issues the evolutionary qualities of aware-ness, values, ethics and conscience through the archetype of the Judge/Oracle. You can discern right from wrong and find the basis of law and justice as well as the inner discernment of what feels "right". Your sense of direction and purpose is here sharpened by your values. It is imperative to discern the difference between cultural values and those of your innate soul purpose. Find out what judgements you carry that are part of cultural conditioning. Differentiate discernment from judgement/blame. Discern-ment simply sees distinctions whereas judgement is charged with emotional reactivity. The number 13 is *not* an "unlucky number", but one that re-quires simultaneous centering and delicate sensitivity to boundaries.

As 13, the foundation stone is cosmic law and awakening your own conscience. In three dimensional form it is represented by the close-packing of spheres (12 around 1) symbolizing the 12 Apostles around Christ or your own capacity to stand in the center of 12 qualities (in yourself or others) and harmonize differences with conscience. The Aztecs had 13 heavens.

The gnomen of 6 spheres meeting in a central sphere indicates the 6 steps of finding what cosmic law is as it acts within your own conscience.

22

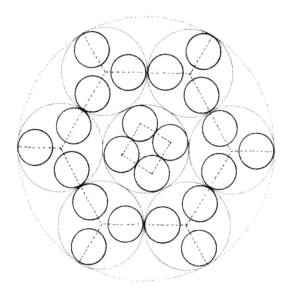

keynote of F''''

In the New Earth, the number four first appears as number 22, relating to the Kundalini archetype. The only *process* archetype among the fours (all others being sources or effects), it relates to the energetic changes that come about when your purpose is lived. As the fourth step in the sacrifice cycle, 22 is the energetic and physical evidence of your commitment to living the truth. There is no turning back with this number. You are committed to your destiny, however difficult at times that may be. 22 implies unconditional surrender to the divine sources.

If you have 22 in your birthdate or name, it indicates that you must go through an initiatory process. In other words, you will be transformed through a powerful co-mingling and quickening of qualities of subtle energy and light through the foundation of your skeletal and nervous systems, which are inscribed with past life imprints.

22 represents the fourth stage of initiation, corresponding to the Mithraic *Leo*, the Lion as time, change and death. In Mithraic art it is represented by the coiled serpent of cyclic energy. The fourth Mithraic Initiation is ruled by the planet Mercury, the caduceus and corresponds to Wednesday. In Catholic sacrament it corresponds to *Extreme Unction*.

31

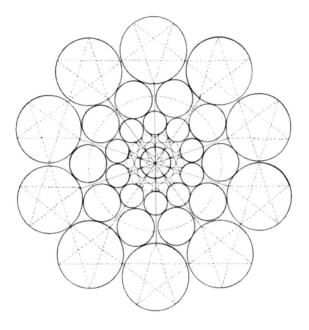

keynote of Cb''''

The four of eschaton is 31, the number of compassion. If you have 31 in your name or birthdate, your destiny has the potential to be a part of the fulfillment of the New Earth. This implies being with others empathetically and being able to receive everything that happens with a wholehearted embrace. It is important to not hesitate in the face of suffering, but to go through every obstacle with a sense of love and compassion even for those who do you harm or cause pain to those you love. You have the capacity to transform the poisons of the world into medicine through your loving heart. Healing through any means whatsoever is possible.

31 represents the 7th and last stage of initiation called *Pater* (Father) in the Mithraic rite. The quality is a steady spirituality and teaching compassion by example. This corresponds to the Catholic *Holy Orders*, the planet Saturn and the last day of the week: Saturday. 31 is the last number in the *Gaia Matrix Oracle* within the Eight Worlds.

FIVE

Fives relate to constancy amidst change, the spiritual meaning of transformation itself. The unequal polarity of two (even=female) and three (odd=male) creates change. Five is the number of the senses and the whole perceptual world. Five is also the quintessence number relating to *aether* or *akasha* wherein the records of the universe are stored. Five is the number of the spirit: the principle that causes change, but does not change itself. It is also the number related to the Golden Section, *phi*—for the pentagon reveals this harmonious and irrational proportion (1: 1.618). Phi is an "irrational" principle that brings about changes in nature's forms.

Five is a number of the fiery spirit in involution—expansive, true and free (5 Immortals). In evolution it is also expansive, ever mixing, separating and combining in the alchemy of the elements. Five represents all five elements in evolution (14 Alchemist). When the elements are fused in sacrifice, there is an opening of the music of all the planetary spheres (23 Music of the Spheres). Five in the phase of eschaton is not in the present matrix, but represents the higher octave Immortals and Burning Buddha, the flame of the spirit fully consumed (32).

5

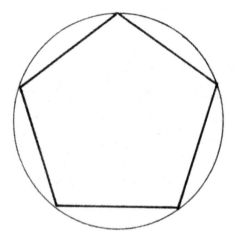

keynote of E″

Five is the second synchronic number, representing a polarity between the numbers 2 and 3. The 5 of involution is the root and ground of your intention, and relates to your ability to be consistent in not only receiving intuition and inspiration, but in following them in daily life. As times change, everything around you, and you yourself, will undergo change. Then remember your vow and be true to your vision. The number 5 resonates to the androgynous spirit within you (5 Immortals).

5 is clearly related to the pentagram and the gnomen of two spheres around one.

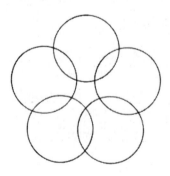

14

keynote of Bb'''

The number 14 in the evolutionary cycle involves inner change of such a quality that you find the alchemical "gold" within you (14 Alchemist). You have the capacity to see, to discern, sift and combine in ways that can bring about your own integrated self. Whatever inspiration you receive you must interiorize as a constant within you and make part of your ordinary life. Strengthen your self-confidence by refusing to throw your power away to authorities. Cease yielding to the expectation of others—no matter how well meaning they are. You can stand on your own feet and transform your life from the inside out.

Allow yourself a 14 day period of gestation for any project of significance. In Egyptian mythology, the 14 parts of Osiris' body relate to half a lunar cycle (waning moon) symbolic of a *change from outer to inner focus*. Deep inner work is required in this lifetime if you have 14 in your name or birthdate.

14 relates to the second stage of Initiation, that of the Mithraic *Cryphios*, the Veiled One. It corresponds to Monday and the Moon. The corresponding Catholic sacrament is *Confirmation*.

51

23

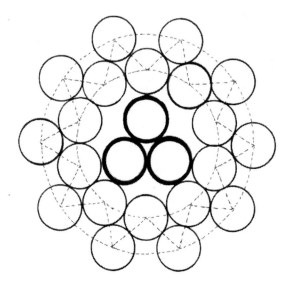

keynote of F#''''

The five of sacrifice in the New Earth is 23, relating to the archetype of the Music of the Spheres—how harmony works through the vibrational qualities of the universe. You can experience everything as change in specific harmonic orders that reveal the patterns behind the plants, crystal, animals, and human beings on Earth. You can attune to the sun, planets, and stars as vibrational qualities that speak to you through a music that inspires you to compose, sing, or make art. The number 23 enhances a gathering of nature into archetypal qualities that can be experienced as the harmony of the world.

23 relates to 11 spheres around the earth as a movement of harmonies in a gnomen. With this number you will be able to relate to the planetary spheres in a sensitive way that will enhance your growth.

Bode's Law and the 12 ratios of the chromatic scale are also indicators of these harmonies.

Bode's Law:

Beginning with 0, followed by 1, we double each successive number in the following manner:

0	1	2	4	8	16	32	64	128

Then we multiply each number by 3:

0	3	6	12	24	48	96	192	384

Finally, we add 4 to each number:

4	7	10	16	28	52	100	196	388

The last row of numbers corresponds closely with the relative distances of the planets from the sun, using the distance from earth to sun as 10:

3.9	7.2	10	15.2	26.5	52	95.4	192	307

SIX

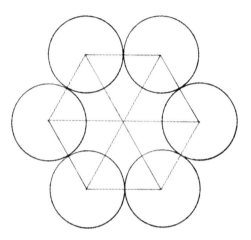

Six is the second cyclic number and relates to either the union of opposites or their conflict. Like fire and water, female and male, six is a complex polarity that cycles from the desire to exist as a separate individuality and yet one that is inextricably bound up with its source and unity.

In involution six represents the conflict of the soul over desires, thereby making the wheel of love go around (6 Antagonists). In evolution, six becomes the solar hero, the incarnation of the golden energies that rectify wrong in society (15 Hero/Demon). It is not until the phase of sacrifice that six is realized to be the sun in the heart, the Grail as a heart and mind in complete resonance (24 Grail Mother). The number 33 is not in the GMO but is the eschaton Antagonist and Eagle-Crooked Path, as the highest octave of love.

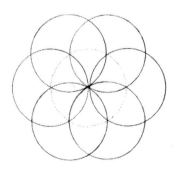

6

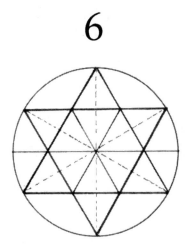

keynote of G″

If we use 3 as a male number, then two threes create a duality of male energy. Hence the 6 of the Antagonist's archetype that derives from a conflict in the soul between love and desire. Love relates to the androgynous nature of the spirit as number 5; whereas 6 implies a recognition of the relative nature of the soul with its own desires that are apart from the spirit's intention and purpose. The number 6 then reveals a focus on the cycles and gyrations of the soul as it polarizes between purpose and the allurements of the world. Consequently, if you have sixes in your name or birthdate, you have the possibility of working through all the cycles of the soul—from desire and frustration, through pain and anger to even hatred, bitterness and denial—then realizing that soul conflict comes from departure from your spirit's intention.

Nicomachus called the 6 "the form of form, the only number adapted to the Soul, the distinct union of the parts of the universe, the fabricator of the Soul, also Harmony." In Genesis there are six days of creation and when the angel Gabriel presents to the Virgin a flower, it is a six-petalled lily.

6 is called "the perfection of parts" by Pythagoreans because it is formed by the multiplication of the first odd number (beyond one) and the first even number. 2 X 3 = union of male and female. The 6 of the Seal of Solomon is the union of the fire and the water.

15

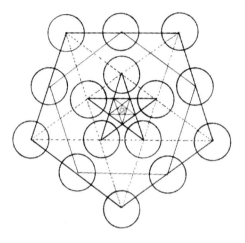

keynote of B'''

The number 15 is a vibration symbolic of having already worked through soul conflict. If you have a 15 in your name or birthdate you now can work out the conflicts of society through the Hero(ine)/Demon archetype. This implies you can be an effective community worker or organizer. Most specifically you can see how to rectify social injustices and can actually implement ways to do so. You do well to understand collective shadows as forces that mirror individual conflicts and to appeal to people's honesty in facing them whenever possible. Your destiny involves the destiny of the family, community, or nation to which you feel you belong. Focus on understanding whether people (yourself included) are coming from personal desire or the common good. Try to inspire ways that society as a whole can be cared for. Keeping things in perspective as well as having the courage to speak out and act when necessary are both essential.

As 3 pentagons (one inside the others) 15 represents 3 phases of developing the 5 senses and perception: 1) simple sensation, 2) perceiving objects of desire, and 3) seeing the inner essence or soul quality. Through inner resonance you can see what is happening in relationships, community or society as a whole.

As a triangular number, 15 emphasizes the 5 senses (as its base), integrated with the Tetractys (10) discussed above. 15 is also a gnomen of 7 around 1.

24

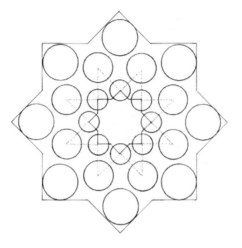

keynote of G″″

The number 24 is the only *source* archetype among the sixes (6 is an agent and 15 a process). Consequently, if you have 24 in your name or birthdate, you can initiate a unity of contraries through your own heart-mind unity. The archetype in the New Earth phase of sacrifice is the Grail Mother. If you have a 24 in your name or birthdate you have the capacity to control the wandering Trickster mind with attention on breath and heart. Conflicts often arise from a mind that leaps ahead, trying to fix the future before it has arrived. Those with 24 can cure this anxiety by harmonizing thought with feeling and coming back to the present moment. Attention on breath in meditation is a good way to do this. Let your heart be your guide—not as every change of feeling that comes along—but the heart that is at the core of your destiny and that is constant. Being open and receptive is part of this process.

The number 24 represents the fifth stage of initiation called *Perses*, the Mage or Adept in Mithraic rite corresponding to *Holy Communion* in Roman Catholicism. Relating to the planet Jupiter and Thursday, the emphasis is on expanded perception by making oneself a receptacle for receiving inspiration. By becoming a cup of communion you can face and dissolve fears rather than slay the fearful images you project (Perseus slaying the Gorgon, Theseus slaying the Minotaur and all the "Dragon" slaying myths).

SEVEN

Seven is the final teleos number of the nine numbers. It represents a wholeness of vibratory powers through the *addition* of the four elements to the three principles just as twelve does as a wholeness of their *multiplication*. As the number of colors in the rainbow, of primary "visible" planets in our solar system and of dominant metals—seven is the number that could be said to be the 'verb' or Word of the cosmos. It activates and animates all things.

Seven guides the purpose of the whole archetypal chain of numbers. In involution, it becomes embodied in the pattern of the human image, the multiple bodies and chakra system (7 Primal Pair). In evolution, the Virgin purifies herself and realizes the purpose of life (16∂ Virgin/Child). This means a cognition of the unity of the Tree of knowledge and Tree of Life. The Tree of Life stretches across the abyss that separates the Old Earth and the New Earth. The 16Ω Celestial Earth is seen by the mind as the purpose and at once the seed, the source. In the phase of sacrifice, seven becomes the cosmic body—feeling empathetic oneness with each and all (25 Black Buffalo). The number 34 is the higher octave of the eschaton Primal Pair and Black Buffalo, but is not configured in the GMO.

7

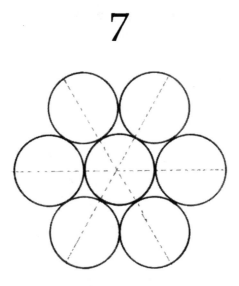

keynote of Bb''

In Involution, the number 7 relates to the Primal Pair archetype as the division of the soul into a manifestation of female and male bodies. Ruled by Saturn, seven is an embodiment of the divine image in the human purpose here disclosed. Seven is a completion in itself, but is medial to the next teleos number of 10. If you have 7 in your name or birthdate you can realize that the body is your primary receiver and distributor, and the body is made up of the four elements (fire, air, water, earth) and three principles (Sulphur, Mercury and Salt). This implies you have a capacity to meld the elements into a healthy body and also a crystallized product.

Most of the cells in your body renew themselves every 7 years. If you have a 7 in your name or birthdate, it implies you are primarily concerned with the purpose and meaning of your life as found in your manifest incarnation—how your soul manifests in time and space.

The pattern of 7 is six circles around one. As the body-centered hexagon, 7 represents the auric soul of 6 in the body. There are seven Amesha Spenta (archangels) in Zoroastrian theology. 7 represents direct cognition, gnosis, and yet symbolizes a blueprint of the whole "body" of the universe: seven vowels, planets, metals, days of the week, colors, diatonic key notes etc.

16

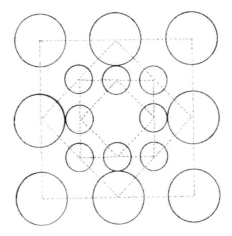

keynote of C''''

16 pertains to the great transition from the Old Earth to the New Earth, which is the purpose of evolution. The Tree of Life stands amidst the two worlds of the fallen and pristine states of being. If you have this number in your name or birthdate it is important that you realize your destiny now, and truly embody it by birthing your whole self.

16 is the only number that has two archetypal aspects as alpha (Old Earth) and omega (New Earth), known as the Virgin/Child and Celestial Earth archetypes respectively. The 16∂ relates to purification of the body to reveal your purpose of birthing your illumined self; whereas 16Ω relates to your wholeness in a pristine state after that birth has taken place.

The Virgin/Child and Celestial Earth archetypes relate to the mystery of the Virgin birth of Athene and the mystery of all virgin births. The 16 as a 7 is considered the Virgin number because, in sacred geometry, one cannot easily draw a seven-pointed figure with a straightedge and compass. It is born from the head like Athene (wisdom) from the head of Zeus (without a mother). The birth of the New Earth as the Celestial Earth also comes through such gnosis.

As a square number, 16 creates the magic square of Jupiter (Greek Zeus, Vedic Dyaus), the high god from whose head Athene is born. Whichever way you add up the numbers of this magic square (horizontal, vertical, and diagonal) they add up to 34 = 7.

25

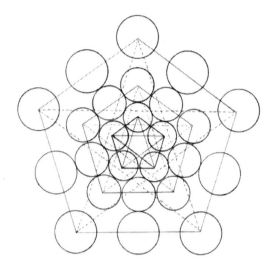

keynote of Ab''''

The number 25 reveals patterns of the New Earth cosmic body in the phase of sacrifice. This is the empathic, expanded body that feels itself to be one with all sentience through the Black Buffalo archetype. If you have the number 25 in your name or birthdate, it implies you can feel how others feel without being entangled. You also have the potential to reveal the spirit in the center of every cell in your body. This gives you the power to magnetize what is within your destiny through empathic resonance. Holding back or refraining from embodying your values will only cause you suffering. It is essential to not only *know* your destiny, but to *live* it by incorporating every detail of daily life into your purpose. 25 implies an expanded energizing of your destiny that can be free of karma.

25 is a square number of 5 X 5 = the magic square of Mars (Greek Ares) the warrior. Adding numbers in any row (horizontal, vertical or diagonal) results in the sum of 65 = 11 (Death Dance). This magic square reveals passageways of going through the death of a corporeal body as revealed in a cosmic body.

EIGHT

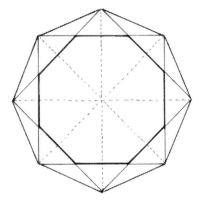

Eight is the ogdoad, a name referring to the primordial eight gods and goddesses. In the Egyptian Hermopolitan Theology eight gods ruled before the creation of the world: Nun and Naunet (primeval waters, Het and Hehet (infinity of space), Kek and Keket (darkness), and Amun and Amaunet (invisibility).

As the octagon, the number eight is the intermediary between the circle as one and the square as four. The octave in music closes the scale of seven. The eight winds or directions are often attributed to this number. The periodic table of elements has eight families. Eight is the cube number of 2, and thereby represents the formal solidification state or the alchemical Salt. In the Chinese Book of Wisdom called the *I Ching*, the hexagrams are all derived from the eight trigrams, which are the fundamental qualities (Creative, Water, Receptive, Thunder, Wind, Fire, Lake, and Mountain) that effect all change.

Eight is the third synchronic number and it vibrates in resonance with the ordinary human mind (8 Trickster). It represents transmission of the previous seven qualities of numbers. In evolution, eight gives birth to new social forms through the individual empowerment and cooperation (17 Synarchy). In the phase of sacrifice, the eight deals directly with the resurrection of the soul (26 Eagle Crooked Path). Like a vertical infinity sign, the eight is produced from the expansion of the soul as it faces shadows. In eschaton, the number 35 is a higher octave of the Trickster and Grail Mother, the elevated mind of the intellect, not shown in the GMO.

8

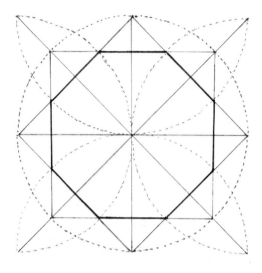

keynote of C'''

As a simple 8 there is integration of experience through the mind (Trickster archetype). The eighth phase in involution is hereby a synchronization of the mind with changing experience. Being aware of being at the right place at the right time is part of your destiny if you have this number in your name or birthdate. 8 also relates to creative genius and quick wittedness and the ability to make precise decisions.

8 represents the first stage of initiation, called *Corax* (Raven) in Mithraic rite and *Baptism* in Catholic sacraments. The Raven is the invisible bird who awakens consciousness as a spiritual birth. Among the Northwest Coast Native Americans, Raven is a Trickster who insures that those he plays tricks on are awakened and quick-witted.

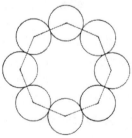

17

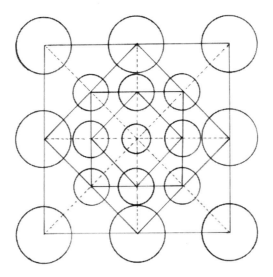

keynote of C#''''

As 17, the number eight stimulates consciousness in general and the consciousness of social harmony in particular.

If you have a 17 in your name or birthdate, you can be part of a Synarchy, a way of socialization whereby each person finds an appropriate offering to a group that is simultaneously a true expression of their own inner being. Perception and appreciation of others for who they are is part of the gift and destiny of the number 17. Grounded in individuality, you can help the social nexus evolve as a holistic interconnection of self-realized persons. Then large networks of people can be managed by trusting the process of each person being who they are. New forms of government in community, business or political arenas can evolve from your inspiration if you have this number in your name or birthdate.

As a gnomen number, correlated with the planets, 17 reaches as far as Uranus, the planet that (unlike all others) rotates on its side, and which is associated with creative genius and revolutionary, sudden change.

26

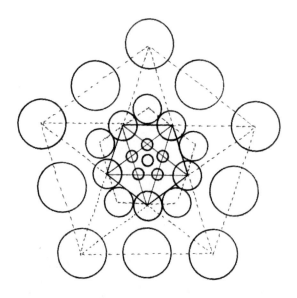

keynote of A''''

The last eight is number 26. The archetype is Eagle Crooked Path, indicating that if you have this number in your name or birthdate, you can completely heal your soul of any past wounding. Acknowledging what you previously denied and forgiving yourself and others will enable you to respond in an expanded way that is completely suited to your destiny. Past emotional conflicts that hindered your relationships can be healed, enabling you to find your own way as a healer, psychotherapist, guide or counsellor. Aspirations—whether in business or love—can be fulfilled and even expanded with this number. The sacrifice is of emotional attachments and addictions.

26 relates to the sixth stage of initiation called *Heliodromos*, the Messenger of the Sun—in Mithraic rite. It represents the meeting of Mithras with Apollo, the sun-god and indicates a maturation of the light body through the soul's power of love and forgiveness. It correlates to Friday, the planet Venus, and the Catholic sacrament of *Holy Matrimony*.

NINE

Nine, the Ennead, referring to a ninefold system, is the final number of the numerical series that we use in GMO numerology. Nine relates to the highest world, related to pure Mind: Nous (Latin), Ennea (Greek), Naua (Sanskrit), Neun (German). It relates to the cycles of experience in the mind as memory. Memnosyne, the mother of the nine muses is a direct mythic descendent.

Nine is the cyclic number that completes the numerical vibrations and introduces the new one. In involution it manifests as heavenly cycles (9 Heavenly Powers) and the birth of time. Nine becomes radiant in the fiery union of opposites in evolution (18 Golden Marriage). Archetypally this nine is androgynous and yet full of surprising change. The nine of sacrifice is a consummation, a burning through of all karma, leaving only the ash of matter and the vibratory spirit that transcends all change. One is then a Buddha, a fully radiant one (27 Burning Buddha). The nine of eschaton (36) is a higher octave of the Heavenly Powers and the Music of the Spheres.

9

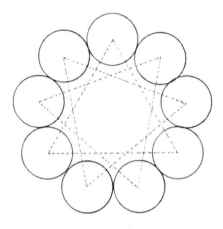

keynote of D'''

The third cyclic number, the simple 9 reveals the nature of cycles themselves through the involutionary Heavenly Powers archetype. If you have this number in your name or birthdate, it implies you have a vibrational affinity for cycles and rhythms and especially those relating to the Earth and the planets. Your awareness of cycles may be lucid or illusory, but with number 9, vision plays an important role. Beholding visions or observing the patterns of the stars may help you see the cyclic nature of life.

The 9 Heavenly Powers correlate to the Greek nine Muses and 9 orders of the heavenly hierarchy, given as three trinities in the Christian Cabala: 1) Seraphim, Cherubim and Thrones and 2) Powers, Principalities and Dominions, and 3) Virtues, Archangels and Angels.

9 is a circular number of 3 triangles as well as the second square number (and the first square of an odd number), correlating to the magic square of Saturn, the god of time (Chronos).

18

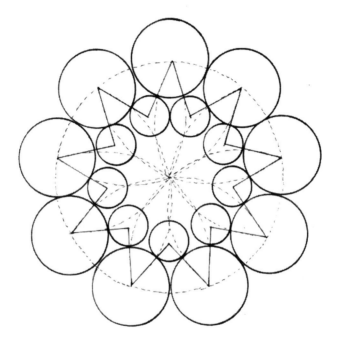

keynote of D''''

The nine in evolution is 18, relating to the cyclic nature of the male and female polarity within you. Sometimes the feminine, receptive space needs to be dominant. At other times the dominance must be given to the male expressive action. If you have this number in your name or birthdate you are charged with the capacity to revolutionize the rhythms of the male and female within you so that you can realize your androgynous nature. This in turn will expand your feeling so that you no longer have an exclusive identification with either the male or female body.

18 is the number of fusion, relating to the third stage of initiation—*Miles*, the Knight in Mithraic rite—correlating to Tuesday and the planet Mars. It takes a warrior spirit to go through the fusion process of the male and female soul within. The corresponding Catholic sacrament is *Penance*.

27

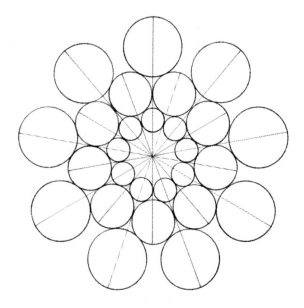

keynote of A#''''

The number 27 relates to the consummation of being in a human body as the Burning Buddha archetype. This last nine among nine as the final number is also the teacher of humanity through the Mahamudra (great gesture-posture). It implies completely burning through karma. If you have number 27 in your name or birthdate, it means you have the potential to radiate pure essence from within, which burns through all limitations, structures and forms that in any way bind you to fate. You are then released to your destiny.

27 creates a gnomen of 2 X 13 + 1, and 13 is the number of Angels who ruled under the supervision of the seven Amshaspands (Archangels) of Zoroastrian Theology.

Path Readings

Use the Path Readings with the Chronological Method (see part one). The number before each group of paths is a shortened meaning of the corresponding number.

Keep in mind that the meaning of the bi-directional arrows (><) is that each path can be read with either number first. For example, 1><5 is the same as 5><1, so only 1><5 is given.

Involution

1 Void
You are one with the vast emptiness, from which you can create anew.

1 > < 2. Divine Imagination
Aligning your will with the source, you can see the potential of many world possibilities. Imagination and inspiration are great gifts for you to seed what has never been before.

1> < 3. Clarity
Divine creative powers, aligned with spiritual order, bring clear orientation to you. Clarity is a gift of seeing your place in the scheme of things and seeing through others' masks.

1> < 4. Eternal Sacrifice
The eternal source of creation gives everything through divine sacrifice each moment so that you can see the sacred in everything.

1> < 5. Spiritual Creativity
The divine creative source working through your spirit is a straight passage to your essence. Allow yourself to follow inspiration.

1> < 6. Creative Madness
From soul conflict you can reach a source of creativity that can reverse projections and reveal astonishing works. Let yourself dance, sing wildly and the new patterns will emerge from the "madness" as it transforms.

1> < 7. Divine Image

The source of all creation enters your body through the likeness of God in the human image. Get in touch with your body if you want to find **God.**

1> < 8. Creative Thought

Mental clarity aligned with divine creative sources bring your innovative possibilities which you can apply to any aspect of your life.

1> < 9. Deep Sleep

The profound depths of your being are one with the divine sources of creation and the cycles of heaven and earth, even if you are unconscious of it. Allow yourself deep rest.

2. Firmament

Your deep essence is covered with a veil of mystery wherein you are predisposed to change, chaos and flowing movement.

2> < 3. Cosmic Conception

The primal substance of your being is a cosmic swirl of chaos seeking order and orientation in the world.

2> < 4. Reverberation

Awareness of the primal substance as an endless reverberating flow enables your divine attunement through openness to the unpredictable, the uncertain and the mysterious.

2> < 5. Formless Mystery

The infinite flow of the primal substance is an unpredictable formless current that forms the mystery of your true spirit. Accept the uncertainties in your life and open yourself to wonder.

2> < 6. Chaos

The primal substance of creation is flowing in unpredictable cascades and chasms into your soul through your emotional reactivity. Feel it all but cease identifying with it.

2> < 7. Primal Body

Your body has a divine nature and moves from the flow patterns of the primal substance deep in the porous openings between membranes in your body.

2> < 8. Penetrating Mystery

The infinite flow of primal substance is a divine mystery that only your big mind, one with the divine order, can penetrate.

2> < 9. Aeons

When nature's cycles return in cosmic turnings to the primal substance, the continuity of patterns becomes discontinuous, making the transition to a new age you are involved in. Allow spontaneous flow until you feel the emergent patterns.

3. Alignment

You are emerging from a vast sea of harmonic waves from which you can find order aligning your will with the divine.

3> < 4. Incubation

As you orient your life in harmony with heaven and earth you can incubate seeds of potential and create a regenerative spiral in your life.

3> < 5. Spiritual Order

As you align your spirit to the divine order you will be clearly oriented in your life, and have the fire of spirit guide you.

3> < 6. Disorientation

The hierarchic order of divinity is a clear orientation that you have departed from through emotional reactivity. This can be transformed by acknowledgement and a loving step-by-step release of old emotional patterns.

3> < 7. Microcosm

The recursive orders in the plan of the human body create a resonant microcosm at one with divinity. You can see the whole universe in your own body. Observe metaphors and correspondences of inner and outer.

3> < 8. Programming

Orienting your life in accord with precise divine orders makes possible new programs for your thinking. Imagine what you have never imagined before and realize how old programs that are no longer useful can be changed.

3> < 9. Vibrational Orders

The cosmic vibrations move in cycles and you can find vibrational orders in your own body, mind and spirit that correspond to rhythms and cycles of nature.

4. Depth and Darkness

You are one with the obscurity of the depths which can enhance your power of attunement by quiet listening.

4> < 5. Communion

The harmonization of the divine through your spirit is bringing you closer to real communion. Through communion you will have powers of vision open to you.

4> < 6. Distraction

Soul conflict and emotional reactivity are a distraction to your capacity to see clearly. Make a practice of going for a walk, meditating, and listening. Realize that emotional turmoil can be transformed to clarity when you keep wanting to know the truth.

4> < 7. Improvisation

As you attune to divine sources you can allow your body to dance, make music or act from deep, spontaneous, innate knowing. Create new situations and enjoy life from a playful vantage.

4> < 8. Meditation

As you allow your mind to rest in divine attunement you become one with spiritual sources. Concentrate simply on your breath and let your ceaseless thinking go. Flowing with what is happening without attachment will help you practice this path.

4> < 9. Sacrificial Rituals

The cycles of nature respond to your divine attunement when you see the sacred in daily life activities. Get in touch with the sacred in your daily rhythms.

5. Spirit

Deep in your being is your spirit which is one with the spiritual essences of all universes. This you can rely on, as the source of true gnosis (knowing).

5> < 6. Tension

Your emotional soul conflicts create a necessary tension with your true spirit so that you can experience your individuality. Allow the tension to bring you to the inherent power of being who you are.

5> < 7. Magnetism

The image of divinity in your body in alignment with spirit creates subtle magnetism that is a power you can unfold as charisma. In time you can develop a spiritual antenna for discerning your direction.

5> < 8. Contemplation

When your mind is clear you will naturally reflect pure spirit in it. Like the sun reflected in a lake, your spirit transcends and yet reflects on your mind.

5> < 9. Visionary Rituals

As true vision rises on the wings of your spirit you will see how to bring inspiration down into cycles of nature in ritual actions. Daily rhythms are part of your destiny when you follow your clearest ideals.

6. Separation

In your soul lies a fear of separation from all you desire, but this is an opportunity to experience the root of your identity, and take steps to actualize who you are.

6> < 7. Conditioning

Insofar as your emotional centers are not balanced, your soul conflict has a prolonged effect on the habits of your body. This could mean addiction or else freedom from such compulsive habits—depending on your capacity to integrate body and soul through deep self-acceptance.

6> < 8. Delusion

Emotional reactions may distort your mind so that you project what you deny. This can be transformed by going back to the root and origin of any suffering and taking steps to remember and forgive. Delusion can be changed to imaginal consciousness when soul and mind are at peace with one another.

6> < 9. Soul Incarnation

The emotionally charged states in your soul have come into time through repeated patterns, conditioning your incarnation. Now that you are involved in your life, you can find your destiny by realizing that you are incarnate for a specific purpose. Keep questioning.

7. Diaphony

Before you were born you had a diaphonous body which you can now contact to align and heal your physical body. Go into the deep structure of the body through both feeling and diet—and feel how beautifully it is interconnected.

7> < 8. Perception

Your body and mind are one seamless reality that are integrated when you both keep open and appreciate the structure of consciousness. You can realize how there is no separation of body from mind when you are sensitive to your body. Experiencing your whole body as a sensory organ brings clarity of awareness.

7> < 9. Rhythms

Your body knows the drum beat of the heart and breath and the rhythms of the cycles of nature in birthing, living and dying. Use music and dance to enhance your innate sense of rhythms.

8. Reflection

The source of your mind is a mirroring of the great limitless source of the universe. Reflect on how everything is made of intersecting waves.

8> < 9. Cognition

Aligning your mind with cosmic cycles enables you to know directly all you need to know. The outer world and inner perception arise mutually and simultaneously when you are open to wonder.

9. Spin and Radiate

The rotations of sub-atomic "particles" and all cycles on earth and in heaven are inherent in your being. As you feel these rotations, you can radiate subtle energy from your own inner being.

Evolution

10. Imaginal
Your creative power is within the imaginal realm. As you get in touch with the great circle of life you will be able to heal, transform and create with great artistry.

1> < 2. Manifesting Power
Insofar as you see the invisible realms of the soul of nature, you can manifest form from matter. Your destiny involves the capacity to transform energy into substance (money, products, and ways of life).

1> < 3. Genetic Programs
The program of all life and evolution can be felt in your own genetic code when you behold life through the soul of nature. Get in touch with nature and speak with the devas and elementals of minerals, plants and animals, and you will feel one with your destiny and inheritance.

1> < 4. Dreamtime
The imaginal realm is open to your conscience when you go deep into the soul of nature. Let intuition be your guide in transformation and realize that your dreams have an intelligence often deeper than your conscious mind.

1> < 5. Holographic Healing
The soul of nature contains an imaginal hologram of your perfected being which you are growing towards. As you integrate opposites, you will find expansive possibilities emerge out of the smallest things in life. You can reconcile irreconcilables and actualize the reality of your true self.

1> < 6. Ecological Reformation
You are part of a reformation of society so that humanity can be part of a holistic ecology. Allow your perception of nature to include culture. Observe nature's network and see how it can be applied to society in similar yet extensional ways.

1> < 7. Virtual Crossing
The pedestrian zone in the imaginal realm is a crossing on the light bridge of purification over the abyss of reactiveness. You can give birth to illumination as the light that creates the "Rainbow Bridge" to the New Earth.

1> < 8. Utopia

Social harmony can be envisioned in the imaginal realm of nature and be activated through individual truth. You are part of a group that is weaving new patterns of vibrations around the circle of life. By taking action on you vision, you will be both true to yourself and part of a greater society in harmony with nature and divinity.

1> < 9. Lucid Dream

The androgynous quality of your soul is becoming lucid in your dreams and visions. Work with the masculine and feminine images within you and realize how the soul of nature is deep in your own soul through millennia of sexual patternings. As you remain conscious while you dream, you can integrate opposites through your insights.

11. Plasma

The flow of the primal substance within you is becoming dense and is energizing into fire by resistance to materialization. Dance with the substance of your being and the matter of all things.

2> < 3. Growth and Decay

The density and order of matter is a rhythmic flow of growth and decay in ever evolving spirals of life. Your destiny involves weaving together matter and life.

2> < 4. Resistance

Matter provides a ground of resistance so that you can experience feedback on your own actions and know the truth. Conflicts can be resolved by conscience when you cease judging and simply watch and acknowledge what is.

2> < 5. Natural Drugs and Elixirs

When the matter in your body responds to your integration, the neuro-transmitters in your brain release subtle essences that awaken and heal you. Energy is inherent in the substance of your body, which can be used by a sensitive awareness of how the elements work within you.

2> < 6. Order and Dissolution

As your community or relationships fall apart, realize that there is inherent organization in matter itself which is a ground of existence. Even matter has consciousness.

2> < 7. Physical Body

As you purify your body you can be whole and realize your oneness with the earth and matter. Eat pure foods, exercise and give thanks to your ancestors for your body.

2> < 8. Hierarchy

The periodic order of matter is a model of hierarchy that also applies to society when people live from their essence. You can gain insight into the hierarchy in nature.

2> < 9. Love-Death

As you love yourself truly, you can accept death as a falling away of the matter of your body from the androgynous divinity within you.

12. Symmetric Web

You can be aware of the symmetric order deep in the universe that is entering the continually changing forms of life.

3> < 4. Self-Awareness

Your life has evolved as a biological entity and now you can awaken your conscience to know yourself. Allow the "feminine"—sensitive and intuitive—part of yourself to be your guide and you can be a link in the greater harmony between nature and culture.

3> < 5. Herbs and Body Work

Life is full of healing ingredients that can stimulate, cleanse, strengthen and calm you if you are willing to receive them. You might explore plants—herbs—and the relationship of diet to an inner alchemy that can release you from past conditioning and bring about greater self integration and oneness with nature. Body work can help open up blocked channels.

3> < 6. Tribal Dominance

The evolution of life into consciousness brings clans and tribes that need to test themselves. When you dominate you are bound to be dominated. You can help rectify social injustices if you also stay in touch with nature and keep yourself in health.

3> < 7. Macrocosm

Life evolves so that consciousness can be purified to see source. With your purification and wholeness you can realize that all of nature is a macrocosm. Observe both patterns and change, structure and fluidity until you feel so in touch with your mercurial, fluid, nature that you can follow through on your vision of a New Earth.

3> < 8. Social Mutation

Life is evolving towards social groups so that collective consciousness makes possible a mutation of culture. You are part of a wave of possibilities that weaves together nature and society entirely naturally. Live and let live, but also cooperate.

3> < 9. Bisexuality

All of evolution polarizes in male and female in order to unite on new levels of awareness and you can now experience the inner marriage.

13. Prayer

Your attunement to divinity is profound when you open your conscience and ask what is true. Invoke what you need and be grateful for what comes. Cease judgement and let discernment of the true and false be your guide.

4> < 5. Self-Insight

As your conscience becomes clear you will be able to see directly anything in your life that needs releasing. You will be healed and be able to integrate polarities in a new-found perspective. Stay sensitive and allow processes to happen and you will live your own wholeness.

4> < 6. Provocative Justice

Saying how things really are provokes the conscience of others as well as yourself so that relationships can be rectified. You are a powerhouse of social change if you stay open to others' points of view and take steps to speak your truth.

4> < 7. Light-Bridge Gate

The abyss of fear can be bridged by purity and wholeness when you awaken your conscience to truth. You can cross the unfathomable past by facing and stepping through your own shadows and giving birth to illumination.

4> < 8. Fluid Justice

Social Harmony can come to life when relationships are justified by the conscience of each individual. By being in touch with how each person's sense of values and rightness is different, you can form a well-rounded sense of how each person is related to others in unique ways.

4> < 9. Karmic Justice

The separations in your soul can be fused when you justify your life by the criterion of truth only. The over-dominance of the masculine or feminine in yourself has influenced you in an unbalanced way in the past and can be changed by a revolutionary inner transformation which you then seek to keep constant and balanced.

14. Miracle

Through the power of your spirit you can heal and be healed completely. By balancing elements and moods in yourself you can create an inner alchemy of true integration.

5> < 6. Reforming Relationships

As you work on the integration of your whole being, your own integrity will make possible the necessary rectification in relations. Your family, work group and friends will discover that you can transform social situations for the benefit of all.

5> < 7. Purgation

Your self-integration comes through a purgation of all that is not you so that the wholeness of the new earth can shine. You are a way-shower through your own purification and the birth of enlightenment within you.

5> < 8. Transmission

As the possibility of social harmony becomes a true vision for you, then energy for powerful healing and self-integration is transmitted to others. Your destiny is in part to create Synarchy by simply being yourself and cooperating with others who are also natural.

5> < 9. Integral Marriage

Your integration, through will and awareness becomes willess when the male and female in you are fused. Using fire and water, earth and air qualities, you can separate, mix, boil and fuse disparate aspects of yourself. This is a high art.

15. Action

Any conflicts in your soul need to be felt and acknowledged before you take action, and then your relationship will be rectified. You are a social hero(ine) and can facilitate dynamic relationships among family, friends and colleagues.

6> < 7. Commitment to Life

Identifying with the whole of society is a difficult purification which you can perform through a wholehearted commitment to your destiny. This is to be a New Earth way-shower through cultural transformation, based on your own integrity and light.

6> < 8. Cultural Revolution.

As old social forms become outworn you will see how to rectify your relationships in accord with each person being clear in the context of the whole. Your destiny involves changing control-dominated relations to mutual respect and cooperation.

6> < 9. Social-Sexual Conflict.

The male and female within you is struggling to be united so that your relationships can be rectified. You may feel pain in not finding a perfect match between your needs and society, but if you stay true to yourself by facing and trying to embrace your worst enemies, you will find they are within yourself first.

16. Formation

Your body is still being formed on ever new levels towards wholeness by your purifications. You are a way-shower of the New Earth through the birth of your whole self.

7> < 8. Cultural Dedication

As you purify your life and experience wholeness, this will naturally, spontaneously make possible aspects of social harmony. Your destiny involves staying in your power and cooperating with others who are different, but who are equally willing.

7> < 9. Birth-Rebirth

Your inner soul marriage is birthing the divine child of your true illumination. The rebirth of the wholeness of the New Earth is seeded in yourself and becomes radiant when you integrate the masculine and feminine within you.

17. Vigilance

Being attentive, awake and aware in every moment brings the possibility of social harmony through relationships. The more you discover who you are, the freer you feel and the more space you allow for others to be who they are. Give up placing agendas and roles on others.

8> < 9. Integrity

Social harmony is a foundation for the balanced integration of the male and female within you when you live from the utmost integrity. Acknowledge the "other" within and allow each person to express themselves in a unique way. Your destiny here is social and cultural, buts success depends on your integrity.

18. Fusion

You can feel the pendulum swings of cosmic cycles in your own soul as a potential fulfillment through the masculine and feminine within you. Your androgynous qualities are natural, and they enable you to empathically feel the opposite sex within yourself. Electric fire is your essential element.

Sacrifice

19. Hologram

You can see the holographic quality of the soul of nature when you enter the "eye of the needle" by being true. As you live your truth you will be able to renew life all around you simply by your presence. You are able to ride White Buffalo when you birth truth from the polar extremes of yourself.

1> < 2. Inner-Outer Fusion

The truth of your inner life is amalgamating with the light of the world. Your destiny is to feel the sun in your heart and regenerate the power of love and light from within. Then you can bring subtle energy and light into the environment.

1> < 3. Diamond Body

When you make truth your constant friend and your light-body vibrates true, your very being becomes crystallized as light. There is no going back now. Your destiny is to marry truth and light in you and regenerate the power of love and light from within.

1> < 4. Shock of Truth

As you go through the narrow gate of truth your energy centers will awaken you suddenly to the unexpected. Surrender to the truth only and the cosmic energy will flow through you.

1> < 5. Harmonic Truth

The resonance in the universe is a spectrum of overtones of the fundamental tone of truth. Your destiny involves experiencing the stones, plants, people and stars as music. When you get a sense of this harmony, you can harmonize nature and culture.

1> < 6. Heart-Truth

The narrow gate of truth opens vast expanses which can bring you to heart-mind unity. Your destiny is to become so receptive to truth that you become a vessel of integrated thought-feeling that others can drink from—for there is no lack.

1> < 7. Incorporated Truth

As you pass through the narrow gate of truth you can embody it and realize that your being is one with the cosmic body. You can feel the limitless quality of your own body boundaries and bring empathetic understanding to all you meet—for you are then living the truth.

1> < 8. Soul Truth

As you acknowledge your desires you can love more and experience a soul resurrection through a clear passage to truth. Your path may zig-zag, but this is simply the seamless weave of your soul married to truth.

1> < 9. True Illumination

As the outworn in your life is consumed, your illuminated being can pass through the narrow gate of truth. Your destiny is to consummate what you have gathered for many lifetimes and burn through all karma until only the light of your true being shines.

20. Solar Chemistry

You can transform density and order of the periodic quality of the elements into forms of solar ecology. Your destiny is to open your heart so that the sun shines within as well as without. This chemical change can be made through light, color and flower essences.

2> < 3. Light Technologies

Being in the light, you can see new methods of circulating illumination from the inner to the outer for healing and all manner of color technologies. Your destiny is to attune to color and allow the vibrations to change your cellular vibrations so that your body becomes filled with light.

2> < 4. Chakra Ignition

Your energy centers are being quickened by the influx of solar energy into your subtle body. Color can harmonize and balance old wounds of the soul and awaken you to divine impulse. Surrender to the divinity in the sun behind the sun and work with color and flower essences.

2> < 5. Solar-Sound Healing

Solar energy circulates in all things and as you tune in to the resonances you will discover new methods of energy flow for the benefit of humankind. Your destiny involves finding the correlations of sound and color and working with music and art to heal yourself, others and the earth.

2> < 6. Free Energy Technology

As your heart and mind become aligned and function together you will be able to see how light circulates as a free energy source. The inner and outer "suns" have become one as light is realized to be the currency, the "money" of the universe.

2> < 7. Solar Body

As you realize your oneness with the cosmic body, the infinite radiance of the solar body will shine through you. Your destiny involves a very energetic process of continuous death and rebirth, allowing you to become more and more empathic with all sentient beings.

2> < 8. Solar-Soul Infusion

Solar energy is flooding your soul as an opportunity for you to see blind spots and be responsible for your desires. Your soul can be resurrected through a penetrating vision and courageous action.

2> < 9. Self Illumination

The light of the sun circulates in an ecology where your spiritual life is consummated in a self-illumination. Your destiny is to burn through all karma and fulfill your purpose through a series of death and rebirth that create a new structure of humanity through yourself.

21. Cellular Illumination

The life in your cells is being gradually transformed into light. Being sensitive to the subtle energy and light circulating in your body is a blessed renewal.

3> < 4. Pranic Vitalization

As your body undergoes cellular change, subtle energy awakens your light-body. Being vitalized by pure prana (subtle energy), your destiny will carry you toward complete soul resurrection.

3> < 5. Synesthesia

As your light-body vibrates more fully and you open yourself to universal resonances, you can hear color, see sound and sense the harmonic qualities beyond the senses. You can use this sensitivity for deep knowing and perhaps work in multi-media to reveal this gift to others.

3> < 6. Extra-Sensory Powers

The heightened vibration of your light-body combined with an integration of heart and mind brings you heightened perception. Your destiny is to marry the sun and the moon, thought and feeling in the vessel of your light body.

3> < 7. Micro-Macro Fusion

As your light-body becomes more activated you will experience an expansion into the cosmic body. This means an empathic oneness with all beings, and an expanded sensitivity. If you feel stretched at times, it is all part of the process.

3> < 8. Ascension

As your light-body develops there is an illumination of your blind spots and you can deliver your soul wholly to the resurrection process. Your destiny is to marry your purified and healed soul with your light-body. Matter itself is transformed in this process.

3> < 9. Enlightenment

The burning away of all dross in your life is changing your cellular structure into a high vibrational matrix whereby you can become fully enlightened. A new structure of humanity can be born out of your destiny.

22. Revelation

Discovering your conscience as an organ of truth can awaken all your energy centers so that you can see beyond the ordinary. Surrender to divinity only as the subtle energy and light bring more and more cosmic energy through your chakras.

4> < 5. Dilation

The awakening of your energy centers is quickening your being into a vast opening, a dilation that can bring you into a powerful resonance with the music of the universe. Your destiny involves opening to the harmonies within stones, plants, animals and people—all of life. Change reveals melodic patterns that have inherent constancies.

4> < 6. Empathy

Awakening to the unity of your heart and mind enables you to experience any other being as if you were them, so that you can harmonize your energies. Working with light and love in the vessel of your being also enables your own brilliance to shine.

4> < 7. Cosmic Matrix Mastery

The quickening of your energy centers is igniting you to a full awakening of the cosmic matrix in the universal body. Your destiny is to master the patterns of a universal language inherent in the cosmos as a whole.

4> < 8. Karmic Transfiguration

As your energy centers are quickened your past karma can be transfigured by the power of love in your soul. Your destiny is to totally heal your soul by working with elixirs and patterns—vibrational medicines.

4> < 9. Entering the Light

As you consummate your life through pure sublimation, your energy centers will awaken you to the full illumination of being. Surrendering to divinity within you is a way of letting the outworn be consumed.

23. Cosmic Inspiration

As you integrate your life and heal old wounds you can open yourself to the resonance and music of the cosmos. Beauty is the opener of your heart to the melodic and harmonic patterns inherent in stones, stars, trees and all beings.

5> < 6. Thought-Breath

Attuned to the resonance of the source of things, your thought becomes synchronized with your breath and your heart can know great mysteries. Your destiny is to become a vessel that is resonant with the music of the spheres.

5> < 7. Expansion Spectrum

As you attune to the resonances of the universe, you will experience an expansion, one with the cosmic body and behold spectrums of sound-space. Your destiny is to listen to what people are, not merely what they say. Through your own expanded perception you can harmonize humanity with the planetary music.

5> < 8. Sound Resurrection

As you own your desires and love more and more you can hear the cosmic sound current through soul resonance and be resurrected in spirit. Your destiny is to work with music in soul healing.

5> < 9. Entering the Sound Current

As you tune into the universal resonances and let your life be consummated with pure light, your essence will merge with the cosmic sound current. Your destiny is to listen to everything and reveal the music within it. This is an essential process that can consume all karma with shere beauty.

24. Open Response

The rectification of relationships will bring you closer to a true response to life and your mind and heart can then be experienced as one. Your destiny is to become a vessel, receptive to everything that comes to you.

6> < 7. Going-with-the-Flow

As your heart and mind are aligned with each breath, your deep being knows how to move with everything as it changes. Your destiny is to find new structure and energy out of change. As long as you keep openly living in the moment, you will fulfill this part of your destiny.

6> < 8. Transformation Body

The alignment of your heart and mind is enabling soul projections to be transformed back into love so that you can experience love everywhere. Your destiny is to weave a transformation body out of the harmony between thoughts and feelings.

6> < 9. Star-Heart Awareness.

The unity of your heart and mind is enabling your life to come to a point of consummate brilliance, shining in the darkness. Your destiny is creating a new life out of the light shining from within you.

25. Bliss

The purification you have practiced brings wholeness and when you are whole, your complete being can expand with an ecstatic wonder.

7> < 8. Resurrection Body

The vastness of your essential being is one with the cosmic body and can transform desires into love. Resurrecting your soul is also an empathic expansion of your body. Your destiny is to create a body that is wholly one with your soul purpose..

7> < 9. Spiritual Consummation

The universe is expanding in space but is conserved in the illumination of your spiritual life consummation. Your destiny is to unite your purified spirit with your expanded empathic body. This "stretch" helps restructure humanity to its greater fulfillment and purpose.

26. Universal Soul Language

Social harmony brings forth the universal language through which your soul can be resurrected. Your destiny is to see blind spots and to have the courage to face shadows so as to heal your soul completely.

8> < 9. Plenitude.

As your loving soul experiences the last stages of release of all that is not of your essence, your life is fulfilled. With this plenitude, you can bring soul healing and spiritual upliftment to many.

27. Constancy

The balance of the masculine and feminine aspects of your soul brings a foundation for a constant direction towards full life consummation. You are living as the epitome of a purified, restructured humanity.

Eschaton

28. Equanimity

When you pass through the narrow gates with balance you can become free through wisdom. Your path is in seeing great perspective to the whole circle of life—and knowing that ups and downs are all part of the greater scheme. Caring about others and the Earth and extending this equanimity to others is part of your destiny.

1> < 2. Inherent Governance

As your wisdom increases, you naturally know how to govern yourself, and consequently others will be governed through the harmonization of your being. Your destiny is to let your wisdom permeate into an understanding of the harmonies of the universe.

1> < 3. Design Mastery

The cosmic structure is a recursive, vast, self-reflexive interwoven system that, with your wisdom, you can now see as the origin of a design process. You can bring forth designs from the intelligence of the cosmic structure.

1> < 4. Wise-Love

As you love without attachment you have a perspective on things and can be compassionately involved. The more compassion leads you to involvement in the world, the more you need wisdom to guide you.

1> < 5. Simple Mastery

Your wise perspective is enabling you to see simplicity in everything. Your destiny is to be still and know that all is well.

1> < 6. Grail Wisdom

The humble quester of the light within you will find the wisdom of the Grail vision. Stay centered and know your heart as the Grail.

1> < 7. Flood of Wisdom

The perspective on life you have can take fine discriminations into whole-heartedness. Then you act always from wisdom.

1> < 8. Idealization

Perspective on all the myriads of beings enables you to see infinite being as an ideal order. Your destiny is to realize the relation of the many and the One.

1> < 9. Cessation

The ultimate wisdom of life is allowing everything to cease where non-being stops the world and everything is accepted as it is. Be centered and allow the radiance to do the work. Cease all struggle.

29. Harmony

The radiance of everything circulating in energy exchanges is revealed as pure harmonics. Your destiny involves being receptive to and engendering beauty. Crafts, jewelry, music, art and the beauty in nature are all part of your way.

2> < 3. Beauty

The spiritual structure of the universe is a web of harmony that you can experience as pure beauty. Your destiny will bring you to music, art and the realization of natural beauty. You can work on an archetypal level.

2.> < 4. Flood of Beauty

Love sees beauty everywhere and the harmonics of the universe then sing through eyes of compassion. You can be involved in the compassionate work of bringing beauty into the lives of those who may be downtrodden yet receptive to the flood of beauty in your heart.

2.> < 5. Harmonic Systems

The harmonics behind all universes are founded in complete simplicity where you can see the unfoldment of systems. Your destiny is to live in simplicity with spirit, with an austerity which enables visions of the intelligence and beauty behind all things.

2.> < 6. Deep Humility

The underlying harmonies behind all universes can be experienced through your humility. As you humbly open your heart and mind to crystals, colors, sounds and forms, you will appreciate everything and receive great gifts of harmony.

2.> < 7. Transcendent Immanence

The harmonics in all universes are immanent in all things, and as you are whole-hearted in your life, you can be with all things without being attached. Your destiny is to be empathic and aloof at once.

2.> < 8. Vanishing Harmonics

The harmonics behind all universes are spread infinitely through being into non-being as you allow love and forgiveness to be constant in your life.

2.> < 9. Sublime Serenity

The harmony of the universe resounds in infinite being through a peaceful sublimation.

30. Prismatic Radiance

Your light-body can pass through density and travel through the cosmic structure in rainbows of light. Through death and rebirth you can more and more allow the Light of Cosmic Intelligence to be your guide.

3.> < 4. Ultimate Oneness

As you realize that the cosmic structure pervades all universes you can rest in a compassionate embrace of the oneness. Your destiny is to work with the sublime intelligence of the universe and weave networks of people together. You can effectively work with communications and media.

3.> < 5. Karmic Liberation

Simplifying your life you can release all attachments and move freely through the cosmic structure beyond time. Your karma can be completely cleared in this lifetime if you follow the guidance of the Light of Cosmic Intelligence.

3.> < 6. Invisibility

The great light web of the universe is within all things and, by complete humility, you can accept the mystery of invisible realms and be more invisible yourself. This invisibility allows you to see more of the cosmic structure.

3.> < 7. High Humor

As you are whole-hearted in your being you can enjoy the incongruities of the cosmic structure, your essence and form. You can enjoy the many facets of life with a lightness of being.

3.> < 8. Mirroring

The mirroring of infinite being in the cosmic structure enables you to see at a distance and backward and forward into time. As you see with love, you will be able to wholly actualize your soul purpose by mirroring others back to themselves in a loving state.

3.> < 9. Sublimity
The all-permeating fabric of the universe vibrates in the infinite vastness of non-being where you can experience true sublimity. You can consummate your life through a refining process of sublimity.

31. All-Encompassing Vow
Your awakening and energy acceleration is moving toward immense compassion and a vow to help others. Your destiny is to immerse yourself in this state wholeheartedly.

4.> < 5. Great Love
Your compassion has already brought awareness of unity and now the expression of your love can reach utter, inconspicuous simplicity. Listening to others wholeheartedly, without much comment, can penetrate layers of confusion and clear karma.

4.> < 6. Bodhisattva Service
Humility and compassion together create selfless service. Humanity is your spiritual family. You can help weave the ways that serve everyone.

4.> < 7. Understanding
Whole-hearted living brings understanding when compassion is present. Allow detached empathy to expand your view of life, and realize that all beings are interconnected in often unseen ways.

4.> < 8. Universal Soul-Love
As your compassion is one with all beings you can love through the universal soul. Your soul resurrection is bound up with the mutual clearing of souls near and dear to you.

4.> < 9. Compassionate Void
When you surrender all to non-being, compassion embraces everything. Your destiny is to plunge into the unknown and be willing to not only accept, but to embrace whatever is happening in each moment.

32. Resonance
The music of cosmic resonance is tending towards the utmost simplicity through harmony. As you listen to others, worlds can open to you.

5.> < 6. Utter Presence

Simplifying your life comes from a true humility and awareness of the place of things. Your presence emanates from the heart of the universe being in harmony with your own heart and mind.

5.> < 7. Oceanic Drop

Your wholeheartedness makes tangible the ocean of bliss in which you float, when you simplify your life. Your destiny involves seeing each finite being in a vast perspective of things.

5.> < 8. Great Art of Being

Infinite beingness supports you through your release of all that is not you until you come to simplicity. Your soul is to enjoy the music of the universe.

5.> < 9. Utter Oneness

As your life becomes simplified you can enter non-being without a trace of fear. Be still until you hear inner music.

33. Forgiveness

Your heart-mind unity makes possible the awareness of the roots of old wounds through humility whereby you can forgive and be forgiven. Your destiny is to be open to complete inner healing.

6.> < 7. Ease

As your humility brings out your essence, you can whole-heartedly let go of all that is not sacred in your life. Then everything will be easy. Allow expansion of empathy with others.

6.> < 8. Humble Wonder

As you come into the infinitude of your being you will be humbled and open to unimaginable wonder. Insofar as your soul has forgiven— yourself and others—of past wounds, you will open to this humble wonder.

6.> < 9. Profundity

Your whole being rests on the infinite depths of non-being through you deep humility. Profundity emerges when you refine your life in a detached process of being ground down until you reach the depths of sublimity.

34. Glory

The immensity of your being is far beyond your physical body and is fulfilled through your whole-heartedness. Enjoy the glory of being who you are through an empathic oneness with others.

7.> < 8. Expansion

The whole-heartedness of your being allows a natural expansion of your essence so that you can be with all things. As you acknowledge your mistakes and forgive yourself you will be relieved of great soul burdens. This process enables you to expand your feelings and sense of identity.

7.> < 9. Total Presence

The great emptiness of non-being is filled by the plenitude of presence when you are fully present without attachment. Living in the moment is living in eternity.

35. Wonder

The resurrection of your soul through love is opening to the awe of infinite being. Your destiny involves having a child's sense of wonder while knowing the depths of human soul experience.

8.> < 9. Return

The purity of your being is becoming so sublime that you can now rest in non-being and return to the ultimate source of things. Weave your path with strands of forgiveness and willingness to enter the mystery.

36. Essence

As your life is consummated through the illuminated fires of pure essence, you can enter the heart of non-being. Your destiny is to free yourself of a sense of separateness and to feel the oneness with others through essence.

Appendix A

Relationship of numbers, archetypes and planets

If you are interested in planetary correlations to the numbers and archetypes, you might find useful metaphors in the following correspondences.

1	2	3	4	5	6	7	8	9

archetype number:

1	2	3	4	5	6	7	8	9	10

(planetary order of days of week):
Sun Moon Mars Mercury Jupiter Venus Saturn (Uranus Neptune
                                                        Pluto)

archetype number:

10	11	12	13	14	15	16	17	18	19

(planetary order of associated metals):
Mars Venus Moon Jupiter Sun Mercury Saturn (Uranus Neptune
                                                        Pluto)
(iron) (copper) (silver) (tin) (gold) (mercury) (lead) (uranium) (neptu-
                                                        nium) (plutonium)

archetype number:

19	20	21	22	23	24	25	26	27	28

(planetary order of distances):
Moon Mercury Venus Sun Mars Jupiter Saturn (Uranus Neptune
                                                        Pluto)

28	29	30	31

For example, if your birthdate is a 17, your planetary ruler is Saturn, ruling 17 Synarchy. The above chart may be helpful in understanding the three types of orders relating to the three orders of the planets: 1) days of the week, 2) planetary distances and 3) planetary association with the metals (sun=gold, moon = silver etc.) based on their atomic weights. The three types of orders correspond to 1) stages of initiation, 2) cycles of time and 3) density of incarnation.

RULED BY THE SUN
1 Creator, 15 Hero(ine)/Demon, 24 Grail Mother

The archetypal points of solar energy work through the Creator, the Hero(ine)/Demon and the Grail Mother. As the true self, the Sun is the divine creative one that becomes manifold in the Hero and releases itself from the labors of the Hero through the heart-mind. Sun relates to heart and Self, direct knowing. Have you asked yourself, "who am I?"

On the solar level the divine light liberates the Self from limited consciousness. Light originates in the Sun (within the solar system) and is transmitted as cosmic intelligence. The Hero brings the light into the social fabric through the number 15, and the Grail Mother weaves the light with subtle energy in the Grail of her receptive heart. The Sun returns to its cosmic level through the Grail, receiving the light from the galactic center through the heart (24 Grail Mother). The will of the Hero becomes transformed by her receptivity of the eternal light of the Creator.

RULED BY THE MOON
2 Primal Waters, 13 Judge/Oracle, 21 Blue Pharaoh.

Lunar influences invoke subtle energy, and the formlessness of primal substance becoming at once feeling and self-judgement (2 Primal Waters). Reflective, conditioned, relating, feeling and intuitive, the moon reveals our social connection in the Judge/Oracle archetype. The subtle energy of the Primal Waters fluidly connects all things and makes patterns in our astral bodies which we then judge. Memory and the past are recorded here in conscience (13 Judge/Oracle). Lunacy is possible from the exaggerated imbalance of self-judgement.

Clarity results when we receive and reflect the moon's light and gravitational forces in a balanced state. Sensitivity and vulnerability come from subtle energy which can become knots when imbalanced. Nurturing is needed so that the inner light body can mature. When we are pliable, sensitive and contemplative, our cells heighten their vibration, enabling us to release distorted judgements, recorded as memory in the DNA of our cells. We need a very nurturing and safe environment to incubate the transformation of the dense body into the light body through the light of the moon (21 Blue Pharaoh). Self-expression, not public show, is important. Birthing the essential self is the issue here. The intake of clear, vital water is beneficial in this process as is swimming and bathing or reflecting by rivers, waterfalls and lakes.

In summary, our social nature opens through the lunar quality of relationship. The creative flow of life from the Primal Waters can sustain the light body when the conscience is clear—implying a clearing of judgement. Communion, delight, flowing subtle energy in the light body will move through the rhythms of life.

RULED BY MARS
3 Kingdom, 11 Death-Dance and 25 Black Buffalo

Through Mars the cosmic axis between the center of the galaxy and the earth is beamed to us. The light of the Creator (ruled by the Sun) and the subtle energy of the Primal Waters (ruled by the Moon) are here integrated as a positive, projective energy. Will, energy and self-confidence are needed to establish the Kingdom and know our priorities. As the warrior, Mars protects the Kingdom, but then the courage of Mars is needed also to establish it.

The Death-Dance is the result of the Mars energy entering matter from the desire nature of Venus (Antagonists). Mars here becomes the machinist, engineer, miner, chemist, and geologist. He becomes the nuts and bolts that get things done technically. Technology and war are the negative side of Mars in the Death-Dance—especially nuclear war. Mars is the flame hidden in matter. The projective martial energy needs manifestation in matter. Action and technology, the dance of matter, comes from the fire of Mars.

But the fire in matter must be returned to the gods and goddesses and to the spiritual world of the Kingdom. It is the archetype of the Black Buffalo within us who can do this. The aggressive, violent nature of Mars must be transformed to empathy for all—whether they have pain or not. Then the cosmos, the cosmic body, becomes the Kingdom. Matter becomes the fuel to transmute the martial energy into empathetic expansion as a refined cosmic body.

RULED BY MERCURY
4 Priest-Seer, 16∂ Virgin/Child and 16Ω Celestial Earth and 22 Kundalini

Mercury is a more fluid aspect of subtle energy and light that becomes the mouthpiece of the divine through the Priest-Seer. As messenger, he brings subtle energy into the world through sacred wisdom, the discerning mind, and sacred science. As educator, writer, scribe, and translator he brings wisdom and love. Quick and changeable, he carries the information of light and power of subtle energy through his nervous system. Very articulate, Mercury uses intellect to translate love and wisdom to us. Communion and communication are his methods. Interchange, commerce, exchange of ideas—are all part of his role through the Priest-Seer.

Working through the 16∂ Virgin and Child, Mercury becomes the child that is enlightened to guide us. Mutable Mercury transmits the wisdom, compassion, joy and play of the divine child so that crossing over the abyss of unknowing becomes a sacred way, enabling the rainbow bridge to the Celestial Earth to be glimpsed and attained. Mercury organizes a guided way to cross over the abyss to the New Earth. In Sanskrit, Mercury is Buddha ("intelligence or cognition") relating to the discerning capacity of the enlightened one. It is through the experience of Kundalini that Mercury brings truth, wisdom and love into a fusion, enabling a release from the unexpressed messages.

Kundalini is the mercurial power of the ancient Priest-Seer flowing through the body when it has walked in the gardens of the Celestial Earth. Guide and messenger, the light and subtle energy are hereby distributed through Mercury into the New Earth through the awakened body-soul-mind.

RULED BY JUPITER
5 Immortals, 14 Alchemist, 26 Eagle Crooked Path

Jupiter is the beneficent king of gods and is the spiritual teacher. Through the Immortals, he brings inspiration, intuition and direct vision. He is the guiding light of the pure spirit. Only good comes from Jupiter. As the planet of eternal intelligence, Jupiter is the pristine, enduring essence of ourselves as divine spirit which the Alchemist seeks to refind. Jupiter is creative because inspirational, giving powers of expression. He is expansive because he works from the deepest inner principles. Intrinsic joy is his guide—which comes through the Alchemist's process of refinding the eternal spirit within and integrating it into total life. Jupiter brings divine grace in the midst of the trials and experiments of the Alchemist.

The full expansion of Jupiter is revealed in Eagle Crooked Path when there is a forgiveness of the hurts of the soul. Jupiter is here the inner guide to discovering the shadows of the soul, giving the beneficent confidence to acknowledge them so that forgiveness is possible. This forgiveness releases the soul back to its inner essence as pure love in the spirit. Thus the Eagle brings clear vision, the power to fly, and a grounded expression.

RULED BY VENUS
6 Antagonists, 12 Life-Mother and 23 Music of the Spheres

Venus brings the love of the pleasure of the senses, the desire nature and sexuality which is the root issue in the Antagonists—for they fight over desire when it falls away from pure love. Venus brings beauty, but also vanity and superficiality through pleasure. As seductress, Venus drives the Antagonists to fight—for she brings frustration of desire as much as she brings pleasure.

But as Life-Mother, Venus brings fertility as well as the realms of the beauty of nature. The desire of sexuality is here fulfilled and births the many forms of life.

In the Music of the Spheres, Venus brings out her love of gems, color and music as well as the harmony of qualities that the Life Mother weaves. Her astral influence on the desire body is here raised to the realization of harmony in all realms. Even bliss and ecstasy can be experienced through her influence in the Music of the Spheres. Venus works here as the divine artist or musician.

RULED BY SATURN
7 Primal Pair, 17 Synarchy and 27 Burning Buddha

Saturn works through the polarity of the physical body as structure, brought about through limitation and contraction. The soul is contracted in the Primal Pair into a finite human body. That the human body grows old, dies, and falls apart is part of the Saturnian influence. Destruction is a counterpart to creation. Saturn creates structure and also returns structure to impermanence. The realization of our physical limitations enables us to make sacrifices when we work with a greater whole as in Synarchy where each person is empowered and confident enough to see what needs to be done—even if it is to hold back one's self-expression. Saturn retards, holds back, tests, to make sure the greater whole is served. Sometimes poverty and deprivation aid us in relating to a greater collective in humility.

Saturn works in the Burning Buddha as a grinding, polishing and refining influence. As the planet most relating to karma, Saturn takes away what is not truly of our essence. He may help bring about Burning Buddha by degenerative diseases, proving the ephemeral quality of the body as the Primal Pair. Burning Buddha is the opposite of a miser which Saturn helps to create. This miserly quality is wholly destroyed in the Burning Buddha. Selfishness as the lower aspect of Saturn has no place in the Burning Buddha. Wealth, material values, our bodies themselves—here are all destroyed. Saturn is not the spirit that endures, but he helps reveal it by destroying the transient and ephemeral. From Saturn's doubt comes gnosis. Saturn also gives the discipline to break through the body to the illumined state. The Burning Buddha then transcends Saturnian fate.

Other Golden Point Products
by Rowena Pattee Kryder

Gaia Matrix Oracle cards
108 cards (44 in color, 64 in b/w)
ISBN 0-9624716-0-7
$33.

Gaia Matrix Oracle book
288 pages, illustrated, 8 1/2" X 11"
ISBN 0-9624716-1-5
$22.

The Faces of the Moon Mother
80 pages, illustrated
ISBN 0-9624716-2-3
$9.

Song to Thee
with Passages and Interspace
VHS video
$39.95

Tree of Life
and Art of Tree of Life
VHS video
$39.95

Cosmic Voices
3 audio casettes
$29.95

Set of 10 Greeting cards
$10.

Golden Point
P.O. Box 940
Mt. Shasta, CA 96067